# The Last Steam
# Railroad in America

# The Last Steam
# Railroad in America

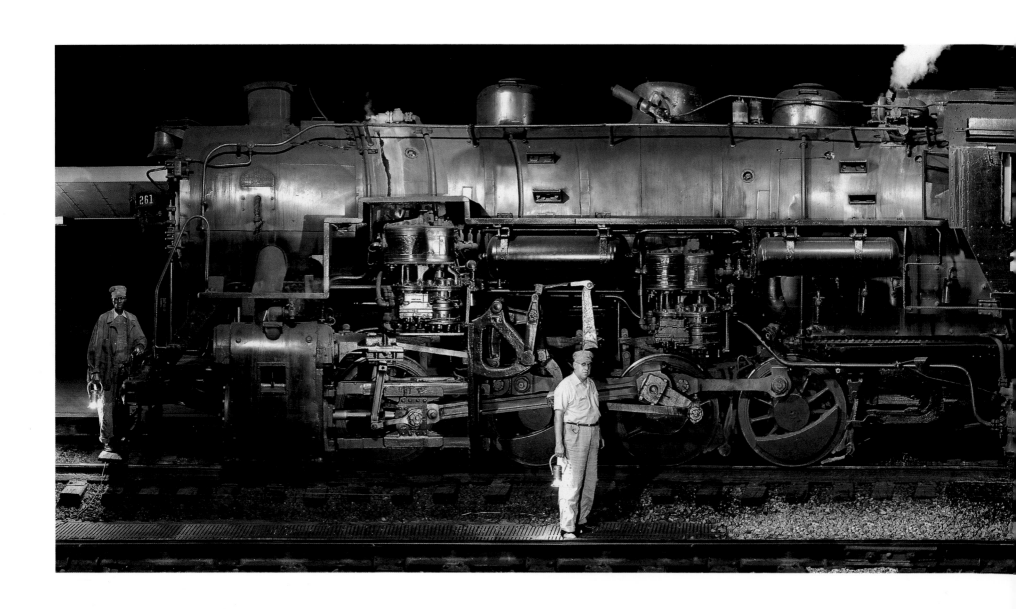

# Photographs by O. Winston Link

## Text by Thomas H. Garver

ABRADALE PRESS

HARRY N. ABRAMS, INC., PUBLISHERS

The Library of Congress has cataloged the Abrams edition
as follows:
Link, O. Winston, date.
The last steam railroad in America /
photographs by O. Winston Link;
text by Thomas H. Garver.
p. cm.
Abradale ISBN 0–8109–8201–3
ISBN 0–8109–3575–9
1. Norfolk and Western Railway Company—Pictorial
works. I. Garver, Thomas H. II. Title.
TF25.N77L545 1995
385'.0975—dc20      95–7406

ENDPAPERS AND TITLE PAGES: The S1a was a class of
powerful switch engines used by the Norfolk & Western and
built in the late 1940's and early 1950's either in the
N&W's East Roanoke Shops or by the Baldwin locomotive
works. They were the last main line steam locomotives built
in the United States. In seven negatives seamlessly pieced
into a single print, Winston Link created a portrait of
Baldwin-built S1a No. 261 and its crew in December,
1958. (NW 1980–1993)

RIGHT: *Class A in a Hurry.* (NW–2128)

Editor's note: the NW numbers at the ends of captions
are the photographer's negative numbers

Second Abradale reprint 2002

# CONTENTS

# PROLOGUE: 1955–1995

*We photographers deal in things which are continually vanishing, and when they have vanished, there is no contrivance on earth which can make them come back again. We cannot develop and print a memory.*

Henri Cartier-Bresson, *The Decisive Moment,* 1952

By all rights, these photographs of the Norfolk and Western Railway should never have been made.

O. Winston Link worked as a commercial photographer for more than forty years, serving his clients by providing them with photographs that answered their needs. The body of work he created documenting the last days of steam railroading on the Norfolk and Western Railway stands as a singular exception to the rest of his career. It was a labor of vision, love, and obsession, but was created for no client other than himself, and in size and intent it far overshadowed any other aspect of his long history as a professional photographer.

Trained as a civil engineer but never practicing as one, Link built his mature photographic style from two disparate sources: his work as a photographer for a public relations firm in New York City from 1937 to 1942, and his involvement as a researcher and photographer for a secret military project during World War II. In his first job, Winston learned ways to make highly organized photos look spontaneous. He discovered how to create images that were so spectacular that no photo editor could resist them, but at the same time contained subliminal messages for his client's goods or services. Later, during wartime, he perfected the skills, knowledge, and patience required to create precise visual documents of scientific information, sometimes even being called upon to photograph phenomena that heretofore had been regarded as unphotographable.

Following the war, Link established himself as a freelance photographer, available for hire. It was his job to transform the often vague and sometimes inchoate instructions of his clients into photographs that were both exciting and understandable. He was an excellent commercial photographer, but the images he made for his clients were not created either as works of art or as records of cultural preservation.

Yet Winston Link burned to do more than just provide his clients with excellent photographs to their specifications. Even before he became an independent photographer, Link dreamed of creating his own theater of light and drama, and doing it with the great locomotives of a steam railroad. His monumental document of life along the Norfolk and Western Railway began as a passionate and personal record of an outmoded but not yet historical technology. It was created using a manner of photography that had also come to be regarded as outmoded, if not actually antithetical to photographic "truth." As a result, it was decades after its creation that this record of the last days of steam power on the N&W was recognized as a technical and artistic achievement of the first order.

Winston Link is a photographic storyteller. It doesn't matter if the story to be told involves bathing beauties from Florida in swimming suits in Times Square asking directions from a New York policeman, the record of some arcane scientific experiment, a cluttered factory floor that had to be made to look orderly, or the essence of a great railroad. Link's photos pique one's curios-

Electrician's helper J. W. Dahlhouse polishes the headlight of locomotive 127, a streamlined K2, at Shaffers Crossing Yards, Roanoke, Virginia. (NW–11)

ity, as a good story, well told, holds the attention of its listeners. Just as the storyteller adjusts and paces the tale, Link illuminates his photos and adjusts the people within them to tell the best story in the most exciting way. And there lies the problem.

By 1955, when this record began, photography was in the throes of a monumental revolution. It had begun decades earlier, with the introduction of the compact 35mm camera and fast film that could take pictures without supplementary lighting, and often without the subject's awareness. By mid-century available light photography, widely disseminated, stared out from every magazine. The style became one of the commonalities of America's perception of itself. So-called candid photography appeared to have been created without artifice, and was widely regarded as a more accurate and honest record

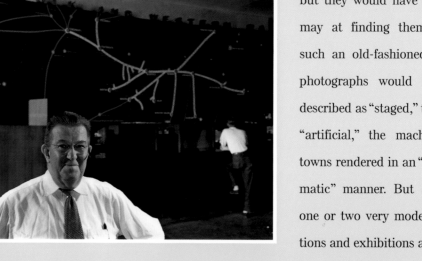

of life than photographs of a more crafted nature, the style which Link had refined with such care for almost twenty years.

This new photography was disarmingly simple. Photographers became watchful strollers. (The style itself was often described as street photography.) The events, objects, or scenes which they documented remained untouched and unaltered, illuminated only by existing light. The camera of choice was small, and the photographer's intentions, frequently even his presence, were unannounced and anonymous. Writing on the work of Robert Frank, one of the great practitioners of street photography, John Szarkowski, then director of the department of photography at the Museum of Modern Art, gave a description for

the whole genre. It was "not in conventional terms tragic, but merely untidy and trivial." It was a style that was profoundly antithetical to Winston Link's philosophy and to his work, for he sought to make photographs that were neither untidy nor documents of the trivial.

If Link had exhibited these photographs at the time they were created, critics steeped in the new aesthetic would have expressed stupefied surprise at the enormous technical effort employed to create these images, but they would have voiced dismay at finding them made in such an old-fashioned way. The photographs would have been described as "staged," the lighting "artificial," the machinery and towns rendered in an "overly dramatic" manner. But aside from one or two very modest publications and exhibitions at this time, Link did not try to share these photographs beyond a limited professional circle. He recognized that the work had to rest a bit while the world itself changed. It was not until the mid-1970s that he began to explore ways in which the railroad photographs might be seen, and not until 1983, almost thirty years after the creation of the first of them, that his Norfolk and Western photos were exhibited in an American art museum. In this time, the hegemony of street photography had loosened, and there was a new interest both in vintage photographs and photographs that were created more recently but in an historical mode, a manner in which Winston Link's work fitted perfectly.

A technical man who enjoys problem solving, Link discusses his work most often in terms of the photographic issues that needed to be resolved. Yet what he created is not simply a technical tour de force. It is a tale of America in which the presence of the railroad serves as the connective theme. Even though the subject is ostensibly steam railroading, there are many instances when the railroad's presence is more implied than seen, slipped into the image as carefully as the secret message in a public relations photo. Often the locomotives are all but invisible in the distant background, becoming subtle but vital elements of this compound portrait of the good life of small town and rural America.

While Robert Frank and legions of other photographers walking the streets of America photographed the country as they found it, Winston Link photographed America as he wished it to forever remain. Yet his are not elegiac pictures. Link created a record of the culture and life lived along the steam railroad as though it would never die. In his photos it has not.

From the very beginning of this project it was clear to Link that its technical complexity and the amount of time that he could devote to it while continuing to support himself through his commercial work would limit the number of photographs of the railroad he would be able to create. He wished to make a complete record of the power, beauty, and wonder of the railroad, including its environment and the people who give it life and vitality. He had therefore to compress into each image as much visual information and personal spirit as he could, while editing out elements that distracted from or conflicted with his technical and emotional program.

The last two decades have seen a growing interest in many different modes and styles of photography. More and more photographers are again using large-format cameras to make carefully constructed photographs. Yet there is a major difference between the thoughtfully composed and precisely rendered images of many younger photographers and Winston Link's earlier photos. Much of this newer work is intensely self-referential, with the marks of unique and individual style expected to be much in evidence—photographs consciously created as objects of art. The art of Winston Link's photographs, on the other hand, is not defined in elements of self-conscious style, for he was utterly unaware of the art world and of art photography throughout almost all of his career. Successful photography for him has always been analogous to those good stories, comfortable tales that somehow coaxed the celebratory and special moments from the matrix of indifference or invisible commonality.

The project of recording the locomotives and life along the line required the vision of an artist who could see what was not there to be seen, either in images that lay latent in the darkness or (like Robert Frank) were so commonplace as to pass beneath our attention. Winston Link saw them. They did not pass beneath his attention. His railroad photographs are unlike those of any other photographer. The night photographs—the first to be made

maintained his office on the second floor of the corporate offices rather than the favored top floor so that he could observe his beloved railroad more closely.

Link recalls that: "With his blessing, I was able to do anything I needed to have done to get the picture I had planned. I was never refused and I was never kept waiting when I wanted to see him. He was always kind, considerate, and understanding. I never knew what word he passed down the line, but it seemed to me that he gave me 2,300 miles of track, 450 steam locomotives and all the employees of the N&W to help me get the job done. He was what I like to regard as a true American and his personality was reflected in every employee I met in those years." (NW–1864)

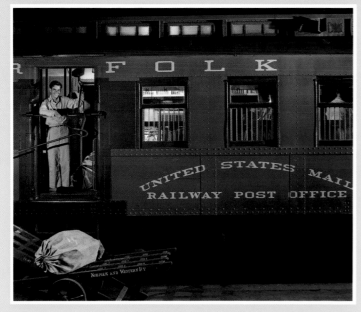

ABOVE: For Winston Link, the faces of the men who ran the railroad and provided its services were an integral part of the total picture of the N&W. He enjoyed showing the employees amid the objects of their work: here he gives as much attention to the lettering and detailing of the riveted steel side of the mail car as to the face of Frank Phlegar, one of the postal clerks who staffed it. (NW–1947)

RIGHT: The Norfolk and Western shared a station in Norfolk with the Virginian Railway, with which it would eventually merge. On August 31, 1955, the station master looked over his paper work, but kept a close eye on the trains from his track level office where a Virginian locomotive about to pull a train to Roanoke can be seen through the door. To the right is a fragment of stained glass window from one of the first two passenger cars delivered to the Norfolk and Petersburg Railroad, an ancestor of the Norfolk and Western. (NW–412)

of moving trains with synchronized flash—are themselves unique, but are only part of his purpose in creating this precious record. Through his background, training, personality, and obsessive commitment to the project, Link was as fascinated by the tough, colorful people of (and along) the railroad as he was by its machinery. His desire to touch the lives he saw before him, capturing their emotions along with their machines, gives this work its bedrock humanity. Winston Link's spirit, which so strongly imbues these images, connects us today with a life that has all but disappeared.

RIGHT, ABOVE:

"Captain" Aubrey Bradshaw, a conductor on the Norfolk to Roanoke run, had been with the Norfolk and Western for 43 years at the time this photo was taken in September, 1955. The conductor is in charge of the train, and Bradshaw reflects this proud responsibility as he stands before his immaculate cars in the Norfolk station. (NW–414)

RIGHT, BELOW:

Engineer F. T. Nichols and brakeman J. M. "Skutch" Stevens, looking every inch the railroad men that they were, pose in front of Engine 382 in October, 1957, shortly before diesel locomotives came to the Abingdon Branch. (NW–1422)

OPPOSITE:

In August, 1956, Buck Stewart was finishing a long career with the N&W as the train announcer at the Roanoke Station. He had an inimitable way of calling trains in a voice that Winston recalled as being "a combination of gravel and southern drawl." Talking so that every syllable could be understood in the large, echoing space, he made the names and numbers of the trains and their station stops roll slowly over the waiting room. Buck Stewart would draw out Luray to "Luuuray." Chicago became "Sheecaago." But he was always understood, and his voice could dominate the din and clangor of trains passing on the six tracks that ran directly beneath the station. (NW–1119)

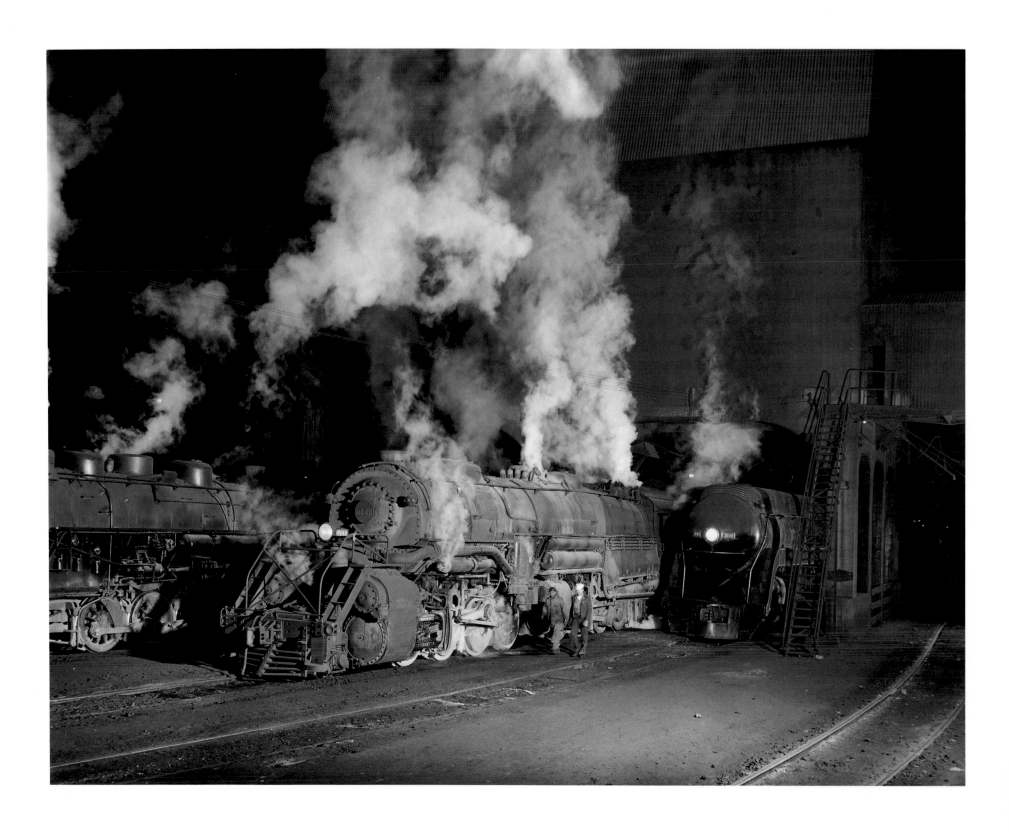

# MAN AND MACHINE OUT OF TIME

From the very first appearance of the steam locomotive in early nineteenth-century England and in the United States in 1830 (on the Baltimore and Ohio Railroad) there was an immediate fascination with its mechanism and a deeply rooted emotional response to its curiously animal movements. Like the horse to which it is so often compared, the steam locomotive's articulations are complex, yet clear and directly expressed. Even at rest, the steam locomotive is "alive." Its flanks radiate heat from the coal fire within and it makes curious noises. The continuous high-pitched hiss-buzz of the turbine electric generator is muted from time to time by the click and thump of the air pumps (and the accompanying panting of exhaust steam into the stack) and the intermittent gargle of the boiler water injector. Whiffs of steam escape from odd spots around the engine, dripping condensate on the tracks below.

Steam locomotives have been absent from the rails for more than forty years, but their memory seems deeply imbedded within us. One may still hear adults point out a passing electric or diesel train to their children, even a Metroliner at speed, as a "choo-choo," thus carrying the image of this mechanism into another generation. One of the reasons the railroad holds such a special place for us must be the size and scale of its machinery and its close relationship with our lives. Where else, other than beside a passing freight train, can you stand within a few feet of a moving object up to a mile long? Autos and trucks are so ubiquitous as to be all but invisible in their commonness; airplanes work either in special compounds sequestered from the rest of life or out of sight high above us.

The passing of the great steam locomotives did not go unnoticed and was documented by many photographers. O. Winston Link was among them, but he took on a job much larger than making a record of the last runs of steam locomotives before they were retired and cut up for scrap. He committed himself to creating a complete document of steam railroading at the end of its existence. This included not only the locomotives themselves, but the men who operated and maintained them, and the social and economic life along the lines that were so deeply influenced by these great machines. Link's record of the Norfolk and Western Railway, the last main line railroad in America to operate with steam equipment, was produced with deep personal passion and at great personal expense. He had to take the time and the money necessary to make these photographs from his work as a commercial photographer, reducing his income and even, on occasion, losing clients in the process.

Winston Link formulated this project in late January, 1955, and subsequently expanded it as his knowledge of the railroad grew. His photographic work on the N&W lasted just over five years, ending in March 1960, a few weeks before the termination of all steam operations on the railroad. The product of this monumental endeavor, the result of seventeen trips along the line, is contained in approximately 2,400 negatives and transparencies, mostly 4 × 5 inches in size.

Just forty years old at the beginning of the project and at the height of his powers, Link had been an independent photographer for ten years, but had been working in the medium for almost twice that long. From adolescence, he had been fascinated both with photography and trains. His father had encouraged him in his interests, at the same time pointing him toward a

The huge steam locomotives are dwarfed by the mammoth coal bunker at Shaffers Crossing that could fuel three locomotives at once. At the left, an S1 switcher, No. 243, prepares to roll into the bunker to take on up to fifteen tons of coal in a matter of a few minutes. Y6 No. 2142 and J No. 608 are already in place and taking on as much as thirty and thirty-five tons of coal, respectively. For this image of locomotives at rest made on a still and very cold December night in 1955, Link used open flash, firing a bank of twenty No. 3 and six No. 2 flashbulbs to light the scene from the right, catching engine hostlers Coleman Hairston and R. E. Hall as they walked alongside their engines. (NW–691)

career in civil engineering, for which he trained. Photography claimed him before engineering could. His interest in trains waned in college but grew again during World War II when his military research work was centered in a laboratory located adjacent to the tracks of the Long Island Rail Road. In his spare moments he photographed passing trains, a practice that was absolutely forbidden in wartime, and it was at this time that he began to fantasize about controlling the lighting in his railroad photos so as to be able to create his own dramatic environment for them.

As Link discovered when making daylight photographs, the sun rarely cooperated and backgrounds were often cluttered and ugly. The only way he imagined that he could control the drama was to use flash at night, and he discussed this challenging idea casually with some of the other engineers working on the military project. Radio control was suggested, but there were too many mechanical variables in such a system to permit precise synchronization of the lights to the camera's shutter. Nothing came of his dream then, but the idea lingered in his mind.

Following the war, as Link began to build his career as a freelance photographer, he photographed trains if they were convenient to his other assignments, but made these photos mostly for pleasure. They had almost no commercial value, although occasionally he might sell one or two to *Model Builder*, a magazine for model railroaders, and to the Lionel Corporation, the leading American model train maker, for use in its magazine.

While he was not very active photographing trains (and has never considered himself a rail fan), Link followed the demise of steam power on America's railroads with great concern. He was well aware in January, 1955, as he packed his equipment for an assignment in Staunton, Virginia, that only the Norfolk and

Western Railway, which passed nearby, retained steam on all its lines. Its major customers were the coal mines of West Virginia, so fuel was close at hand and inexpensive. A careful man, Link obtained an N&W passenger schedule and discovered that if the work on his assignment went well, he might have time to travel the few miles to Waynesboro, Virginia, to see Train No. 2, the N&W's New York Train, stop on its evening run from Roanoke, Virginia, northward to Hagerstown, Maryland, and New York.

The day's shooting did go well, but the trip to Waynesboro that evening was the day's real excitement. A friendly agent manning the railroad station at Waynesboro invited Link to come and look around. Out in the adjacent freight yard, an engine was assembling cars for a freight run; the arrival of Train No. 2 was as thrilling as he had imagined.

Appealing to an acquaintance to help him, Link returned the next night, January 21, 1955, to make his first night photograph along the Norfolk and Western Railway. He used two remote flash units to light the scene. One was placed on the station platform to light the front of the station and platform, the other across the tracks to light the engine and the rest of the station. The illumination resembled what one might see on a station platform, except that there was much more of it. The lights were placed low, emphasizing the shape of the locomotive and station against the darkness.

Link was so pleased with the result when he developed the photograph back in New York that within a matter of hours he created a plan which was to dominate his life for the next five years and more. If the Norfolk and Western would give its permission, Link would finally realize his dream of being able to photograph a railroad at night, capturing images of railroading never before seen. He sent the picture and other samples of his photographic work to the railroad's public relations department, asking for permission to create a series of night photographs along the line that would feature N&W employees. There would be no cost to the railroad; all Link asked was permission to enter the railroad's property.

A few weeks later Ben Bane Dulaney, a senior executive in the public relations department, responded. Permission was granted, the railroad would cooperate, and there would be almost no limitations on what Link could photograph. Dulaney became a champion of the project, which was forcefully backed by R. H. Smith, President of the N&W. An operations man since he had come to the railroad fresh from college in 1911, Smith loved steam equipment and was pleased to see this record created before steam vanished, especially from his railroad.

Winston Link was on his way. Now he was to be his own client, his own art director, as well as the photographer. He was free to make photographs as he saw them, without the need to tout products or sell services. He didn't have to deal with a client who just couldn't seem to understand the way in which he worked. It was just as well. As the railroad itself was operating with an old technology that was undergoing radical transformation, so was the manner in which Link practiced photography.

He was a young practitioner of a style that had been formed and refined for more than a century. In the studio or on location a large camera fixed on a tripod was the standard. The light-gathering capacity of lenses and the speeds of film materials were very slow; action subjects were difficult to control. For most photographs people, props, and lighting were carefully placed and hours might pass before a single image was exposed.

In the early 1930s, relying on the new 35mm films that had been developed for the motion picture industry, small cameras came into use and they changed not only the way that photographs were made but the way they were perceived as devices for revealing the truth.

A number of picture magazines, *Life* and *Look* chief among them, were started in the thirties to exploit this new kind of photography. They created photo essays of candid images, quickly made and sometimes grainy or even blurred. The acceptance of this photography was speeded by World War II where photos made during the heat of battle became the key documents of the conflict, the very best of them becoming icons of the war.

After the war, more and more photographers came to work with small cameras and available light. Advertising agencies and their clients, noting the trend, began demanding photos for their advertising and publications reflecting this new style. Such pho-

Winston Link took this self-portrait as a traveler in June 1955, consulting the schedule in the Roanoke station. The station, redesigned by Raymond Loewy, was completely rebuilt in a spare "modern classical" style in 1949. It spanned the double-tracked east-west main line and was equipped with all the modern conveniences, including escalators to the six passenger platforms.

The station restaurant overlooked the tracks, and Link sat there many times watching the J class locomotives pulling passenger trains into and out of the station. Class As and Y6s hauling great loads of coal and freight rumbled beneath his feet; S1 switchers moved briskly back and forth, making up passenger trains for all directions. It was a train lover's paradise. (NW-297)

At right is Winston Link's
first N & W photograph,
Train No. 2 at Waynesboro,
Virginia, January 21, 1955.
(NW–1)

tographs were regarded as somehow being more honest, as though the images had been snatched from real life rather than being most carefully orchestrated. It was a type of photography which Link used with great moderation. For no matter how clever he was at creating "candid" scenes by carefully setting them up, he was never very comfortable working with a small camera making truly unposed photographs.

Link used a small camera when there were no other options,

but steam operations on the N&W came to be documented with a precise, highly controlled and directed photographic methodology. Here were two antiquated technologies—steam railroading and large format photography—each out of their time, but both so very well suited to each other.

From the first, Link regarded the project as the creation of a complete work of art. He supervised every detail of every photograph, never leaving to chance any element he could control. It

Three months later he returned to reshoot the scene, adding lights inside the station, people waiting on the platform, and more light on the locomotive and second floor of the station in the background. (NW–57)

was always his plan to see this whole body of work exhibited or published as a visual biography of the end of main line steam railroading in mid-twentieth-century America. Later, he produced sound recordings and motion pictures of the railroad to make the experience richer and his documentation more complete.

Winston Link began the project by addressing the technical issues that demanded immediate resolution. He enumerated them early on:

1) Visualizing how a picture might look when illuminated at night, when it could only be seen in daylight.
2) Frequently having to set up and shoot in all but total darkness.
3) Most often being able to make only one shot per camera at any one opportunity.
4) Photographing an object moving at up to 60 miles an hour.
5) Placing this moving object in the right position, often in total darkness.
6) Maintaining extreme depth of focus, front to back, with a 4 × 5 camera.

Any one of these was a problem, but all six taken together generated a real challenge. The lighting was the major problem. Link once laughingly said that "I can't move the sun—and it's always in the wrong place—and I can't even move the tracks, so I had to create my own environment through lighting." Natural lighting was indiscriminate, often unpredictable, and not susceptible to any degree of control. Natural light revealed things that were distracting, and obscured details that were vital to the photograph. The answer lay in creating a theater of light, controlled and manipulated by the photographer.

Link's first photo made at Waynesboro showed the way. He invented a lighting system using flashbulbs placed in key locations. His goal was to replicate the sort of nighttime illumination that one might regard as being normal for a town street or railyard. Using flashbulbs, he fabricated patterns of light that seemed right for every scene, even places far out in the country

A few months later Link returned to photograph Hawksbill Creek swimming hole, one of his best known images. Now the highlights are on the bridges, swimmers, and locomotive, while the river bottom and river bank are deliberately left in shadow. (NW–1126)

and normally in complete darkness after sunset.

Some commentators have mistakenly described this lighting as "surreal," yet it was devised not to create a dream image or imagined landscape, but to frame Link's vision of reality. But because he wanted to dramatize certain parts of the composition through selective emphasis, usually excluding much more than it included, his lighting was decidedly theatrical. This was his intention, for he had the task of capturing the essence of the railroad and the human and natural environment in which it operated in few photos; sometimes just one had to do it.

While Link doesn't recall seeing Carol Reed's 1949 film, *The Third Man*, or Orson Welles's *Touch of Evil* (1959), both movies are examples of lighting used in such an emphatic and nocturnal way. Those films—and the night photographs of the Norfolk and Western Railway—were among the last images of the period created with such a strong and intentionally theatrical light-drama, for available-light images already dominated still photography and were coming to powerfully influence motion pictures as well.

Less than two months after he made the first photo at Waynes-

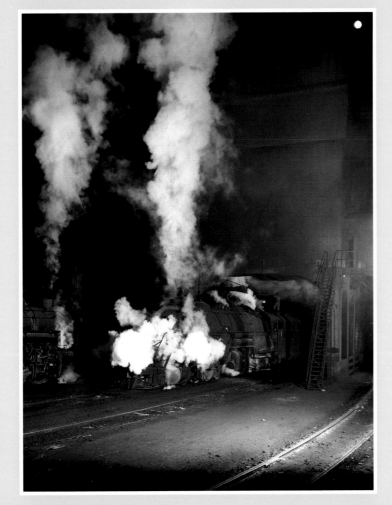

boro, Link was back in Roanoke, Virginia, headquarters of the Norfolk and Western, to begin his work at Shaffers Crossing, the huge and well-kept engine servicing yard just west of downtown. It was logical that he start there for this was an environment of heavy industry, one that he understood well from his work in factories, refineries, and docks around the country. It offered an area of modest size, relative to the whole project, where he could begin to shape his point of view and polish his technique.

These early photos are quiet images; some are almost still life in character, others are carefully created portraits of men and their machines. Link had to get the feel of the railroad, to gauge these objects on the ground glass of his view camera, just as he had done at dozens of industrial sites before this one. This one was different, however. He was making these photographs to satisfy himself alone, and these first few had to fit into the scheme of the entire project—and he hadn't even mapped out what the scope of the project would be. He hadn't even seen all the rest of the railroad. But Shaffers Crossing was a start. Coal smoke was in the air, cinders were underfoot (and on everything else as well) and Winston Link was recording the life he loved.

N&W's fastest passenger locomotive, the 872,600-pound J Class 605, gets washed at Shaffers Crossing in Roanoke. Wilfred Jones, Jr. gives the running gear an extra blast of cleaning solution—kerosene mixed with steam-heated water. Link lighted the scene with one lamp for mood and emphasis. (NW–13)

The locomotive water plug stood adjacent to the wash stand at Shaffers Crossing. Here, a switch engine stops to fill up in March, 1955. (NW–14)

engine and drive wheels of Y6 no. 2180 into position on top of the low pressure engine and drive wheels. This process was known as "wheeling," and was part of the major overhaul all steam locomotives underwent at least every five years. (NW–700)

Foreman Isbell then signals the crane operators to come ahead slowly as the two massive parts of the engine are brought together near the end of the month-long reconstruction process. In addition to the main light source from the left, Link has added small flash units behind the massive frame. This highlighted workers on the other side of the engine and showed another locomotive at an earlier stage of the reconstruction process. (NW–696)

OPPOSITE:
Wreathed in steam, a Y6 glides out of the wash bay in the yards at Bluefield, West Virginia. (NW–342)

ABOVE:
A Y6 and an A face each other in the Shaffers Crossing wash stand, the same location in daylight where Link photographed a J being washed and an S1 switcher taking water that appear on pages 24 and 25. The huge bulk of the coaling tower is just visible in the left background. (NW–1678)

FOLLOWING PAGES:
In the Norfolk and Western's East Roanoke Shops, night foreman W. P. Isbell, hands clasped behind him, watch two cranes move the boiler, high pressure

In February 1959, Link found H. H. Wilbourne in the Shaffers Crossing yards using a torch to test for leaks in the air brake system of a Y6. Reportedly, as little as a quarter pound of leaking air would blow out the torch. This sequence of photographs, made near the end of steam on the Norfolk and Western, illustrates the massive size and scale of these engines. The engine and tender measured almost 115 feet long, with drive wheels 58 inches in diameter. (NW–2089, 2090, 2091)

# THE DOMESTIC RAILROAD

In the spring and summer of 1955, Link methodically rode the railroad, covering most of the 2,300 miles of track that was located in Virginia, West Virginia, and North Carolina. He would ride first on one side of the train, then repeat the trip on the other; his preferred position was in the dining car with a freshly brewed cup of coffee before him. Armed with one of his ever-present notebooks and a timetable Link scouted for possible shooting sites. The most promising would be revisited by car. Two of his best guides were word of mouth and the maps produced by the United States Coast and Geodetic Survey, which pointed out spots where the railroad crossed a remote bridge or indicated other interesting bits of topography. Traveling along the line by automobile was critical to finding sites for photographs, for what might be all but unnoticed from the train could be highly dramatic from the side of the tracks, where he would be making his photos.

At this time, the Norfolk and Western operated with four major divisions, all of which came together in Roanoke. The Radford Division angled southwest from Roanoke to Bristol, Tennessee, carrying freight and passengers destined for the deep south. The Norfolk Division reached eastward from Roanoke to Norfolk. While it carried some passenger traffic, the vast majority of its trains were heavy coal freights, each moving thousands of tons of soft coal to the Tidewater shipping docks in Norfolk and Lamberts Point. The coal was mined along the N&W's Pocahontas Division, which split northwest from the Radford Division just west of Roanoke, traveling up into West Virginia and Ohio. The Shenandoah Division ran northeast through Virginia's historic and beautiful Shenandoah Valley to the northern termination of the railroad in Hagerstown, Maryland.

Most of the sites Link selected to photograph were on the Shenandoah, Radford, and Pocahontas divisions, or in the shops and yards around Roanoke. The Norfolk division, with the exception of Blue Ridge grade, was mostly straight running across open country, which was much less interesting to the photographer than the rolling and mountainous country of the other divisions. There, the railroad often occupied the centers of narrow valleys, with the towns jammed in beside the tracks. This crowding of houses, commercial buildings, parks, swimming pools, and people next to the great locomotives made exciting visual drama on a stage that was of the size Winston could easily light. (Many of the photographs he made along these divisions appeared in *Steam, Steel & Stars*, published in 1987.)

The task he had cut out for himself was monumental, and pressure was applied from another source as well, for shortly after Link started his work the Norfolk and Western began to convert to diesel power. The Shenandoah Division was to be the first to lose steam, so his own timetable was governed by another factor over which he had no control.

Link immediately established certain priorities for his documentation. There were images that he had to have, and his notebooks quickly filled with ideas of how to photograph what he had seen. Link's field engineering training served him well as he sketched out his plans. He made drawings of trackage and buildings, and noted the placement of the lighting equipment for the photo. Often it would take him months, or even years, before he could return to the location to make the photograph he envisioned, but he never left his New York studio for the railroad

without a well-developed plan for what he would be photographing on that trip. On occasion, when he arrived at a site, Link's carefully considered images just didn't seem to compose themselves very well when he set up the cameras. At other times a sudden vision might turn into a very lucky shot. These experiences were relatively rare, however. When Winston Link set up his camera, he knew what to expect, and generally how it would look.

One of the only requests that the railroad had asked of the photographer was that he not make photographs if the locomotive was making excessive amounts of smoke, or if the safety valve was popping, evidence of improper firing of the boiler. Generally, Winston respected this request. On one occasion he even had a passenger train stopped and backed up so that he could make a night shot without too much smoke. Occasionally he overlooked the railroad's wishes, particularly on the Abingdon Branch, where the steep grades made it almost impossible to pull into a station without having the safety valve popping.

While Link had planned to make photographs exclusively at night, it soon became clear to him that there were many wonderful photographs to be made in daylight. Further, certain activities of the railroad, the operations of the Abingdon Branch among them, took place only in daylight, so daylight photos

quickly became a significant part of the documentation. At first, Winston had seen daylight photographs as a way of improving his efficiency. This project was being entirely funded from his successful commercial business, but it stretched his time and finances. As he said, there was no reason to stand around during the day "wasting time" waiting to make a night photograph when there were good images to be made in daylight.

Sometimes the reasoning behind Winston Link's choice of the scenes he chose to document is clear. The graphic power of the twin water tanks at Buena Vista, Virginia, standing monumentally against the black sky, immediately suggested an equally powerful photograph. So too with the great steel bridge west of Cooper Tunnel, which so effortlessly supports the heavy load of a long coal freight or fast-moving passenger train. But what about the somewhat tatty domesticity of the crossing guard's shack elevated above Roanoke's Jefferson Street or the two brakemen chatting on the back of a caboose as a train of empty coal hoppers rolls slowly past the platforms of the Roanoke station? It is images such as these, interspersed with views of the great machines, that give Link's whole endeavor its humanity. Further, these more "domestic" photos are a strong reminder of the size and scale of steam railroading. Not only were the engines and their servicing equipment huge, but the very

scale of individual parts, from drive wheels to wrenches, was enormous. The men of the railroad offered the human measure against which one could read the true dimension of these leviathans.

Winston Link has always been drawn to idiosyncratic personalities, be they human or inanimate, as an extension of his own personality, which is so strongly theatrical. This railroad had such a personality. It was built not only of steel, wood, and concrete, but carried within it the marks of age and struggle and

accommodation to difficult country. There were other, harder to measure qualities too, which Link worked to document by allusion, such as order, respect, and pride. The men of the railroad developed an increasing respect for Winston after they saw that his interest was both genuine and very deep seated. Yes, he was an outsider, but he felt as they did about their railroad, and was truly interested in them and their work. Even the fact that he was from New York City, a location of unfathomable mystery in these parts, was forgiven, and eventually he was paid the railroad's highest compliment. He was given a switch key that opened all the telephone boxes along the line, giving him direct communication with the dispatchers and their up-to-date train schedules. He had earned the railroad's trust.

Without ever having studied art or photography Link had an innate sense of composition. He strongly favored objects in the foreground that established a strong illusion of depth. It always irritated him that painters could adjust the precision of focus in their pictures: the camera was much less flexible. He has said that "what I like to do is get a big object in the foreground—smack you right in the face—and have it sharp. But I want everything else in the background sharp too." This is nearly impossible with the equipment he used. The 4 × 5 inch negative size of his cameras produced wonderful prints, but the long focal length of these lenses gave a very shallow zone of sharp focus unless the lens opening was stopped down, made very small. Stopping down was rarely possible, however, because he needed more light to permit a faster shutter speed to stop the train's motion. There was not enough light to properly expose the film on night photographs and stop down the lens as well.

The large view cameras that Link used are very flexible instruments, however. The lens board may be raised, lowered, and swiveled, as can the back of the camera where the film is placed. Link compensated for the problem of depth of focus by adjusting the selection of lenses, angle of the lens board, and adjustment of the film plane. He was a master of the view camera's swings and tilts, and through these various adjustments he

could produce remarkable depth of field.

Link most commonly used lenses of two focal lengths: a 5¼ inch normal lens and a 3⅝ inch wide angle lens. The normal lens replicated the scene most accurately in terms of the relative sizes of objects from foreground to background. The wide angle lens allowed the photographer to work in crowded situations such as interiors or where buildings or other objects blocked the view he desired. The wide angle lens has a greater depth of field but dis-

torts the size of objects: things closer to the camera appear relatively larger than objects in the background. Spaces also appear larger as well, and as a result the wide angle lens must be used with great care if it is important to preserve an accurate sense of objects and space.

Link can hardly give a greater insult to a photograph than saying it has "no depth." In his own work, he added to the technical achievement of depth of focus with compositional devices. Time and time again, he would position the camera very close to

Winston Link's sense of humor drew him to photograph what he called the "parallelogram house." The building was slowly slipping to oblivion, helped no doubt, by the thunderous vibrations of the huge Y6 locomotives that pulled long trains of coal hoppers past this spot in Falls Mills, West Virginia, many times a day. (NW–381)

The engine crew look out proudly from the cab of their locomotive as Train no. 11, fondly nicknamed the "Punkin' Vine" for its meandering roadbed, awaits its departure from Roanoke to Winston-Salem, North Carolina. The success of the railroad's J class passenger engines led the N&W to cover a number of its older K class passenger locomotives in J-style shrouds, designating them as K2s. These locomotives are identifiable by their 100 numbers and by their less sophisticated running gear. The meticulous maintenance of the N&W passenger equipment is evident in this well-washed train, which operated just one round trip daily on a modest branch line. (NW–394)

the roadbed and very low to the ground, so he could use the tracks as a powerful spatial device to give the image depth as well as movement from front to back, rather like speed lines on the sides of an automobile.

One of the vices of railroad photography, and one which he did not entirely escape, was what Winston called "the wedge shot," the undramatic three-quarter view of a train made by a photographer standing at a 30- to 45- degree angle to the tracks. In these images the front and side of the locomotive were most prominent, with the rest of the train tapering like a wedge to a distant vanishing point. One of the major reasons Link worked to avoid such photographs is that his major interest was not in recording examples of specific locomotives and railroad rolling stock. He had little respect for those who were interested only in the machinery, with little concern for the environment in which it operated. He used to describe their photos derisively as "hard-

ware shots." For Winston the locomotive and train were most interesting when seen in context, and the train's relationship to the environment was critical. He would add people, work with the lighting, and position the camera next to signal lights or buildings to avoid the dreaded wedge.

There is no question that Winston Link is best known for the remarkable lighting of his night photographs, and lighting was a specialty that had won him a number of clients well before he started his documentation of the N&W. He was an expert at photographing industrial buildings at twilight, when the steep angle of the sunlight would create good highlights and shadows, giving the best appearance to these often dreary structures. He might even leave the camera exactly in place until nightfall, exposing the film again when the building's lights were on, turning a factory or refinery's towers into a delicate castle of light.

Occasionally flash might be added to this mix to give life to an area that could be lighted in no other way.

Flash was an integral part of photographs made during daylight, too, when additional light might be necessary to fill in areas of dark shadow. In the time before electronic strobe flash units became commonplace, Link, like other commercial photographers, had wide experience with flashbulbs. Each bulb was filled with a loose skein of aluminum wire that burned with an intense white light when electricity was applied to its contacts. Each bulb could be used only once, and there were many different types available. Each had its own characteristics, including the speed at which the aluminum would ignite in the bulb, and the length and intensity of its light output. Calculating the light necessary to cover long distances and balancing this flood of light against single flashbulbs used as point sources of light in lanterns or interiors took knowledge; Link's engineering background served him well in making these computations.

Link used lighting, both in the studio and on the railroad, in a particularly sculptural manner, to emphasize depth and form. At night, for example, a flash placed a few feet above track level would wash the dark running gear of a locomotive, bringing out in sparkling detail all the articulations that might otherwise disappear in shadow in a photo made during daylight hours. Flash placed to the side or back of a locomotive would reveal the glow of smoke and steam, at the same time outlining the dark bulk of the locomotive against the equally dark background.

Before blocking out a night photo, Link would examine the scene to find the existing ambient light sources, if there were any. He then developed his lighting plan either to reinforce these sources, or artificially simulate lighting that could exist. One of

his favorite techniques in planning night photos was the use of specular lighting. He planned his photographs using one of the basic laws of physics, that the angle of incidence of a light source is equal to the angle of its reflection. Link would aim his flash reflectors at the locomotives, buildings, or other objects he was photographing at the same angle he used for the cameras. The resulting photographs recorded the glittering highlights from the metal of the engines and strong reflections from buildings and landscape. In this way Link added potent highlights to dark objects and got maximum power from his illumination.

Another problem he faced in his effort to stop motion at night was synchronizing the all but instantaneous flash of light with the shutters of the cameras. While flashbulbs had been used over the years for outdoor night photographs covering huge areas, these photos were typically made with open flash, in which the camera's shutter is opened, the bulbs are fired, and the shutter is closed. The problem with open flash is that it cannot operate faster than 1/50th of a second, which is too slow to stop rapidly moving objects. One of the key parts of Winston's plan was to record the trains of the N&W at work, using flash synchronized with the shutter at 1/100, 1/200,

On the evening of September 2, 1955 Winston Link tried an experiment with his lighting systems which he subsequently described. "This was primarily an experimental exposure to include the Virginia Electric Power Company's Reeve Avenue plant [in Norfolk] at that great distance without the use of flash bulbs. The exposure was tested to see if it was possible to overcome the need of radio-controlled flash to illuminate such a huge object at such a great distance. I resorted to a combination time exposure of 3 minutes and flash to solve this problem." Link regarded the results as a failure and set the negatives aside for years until he was looking for a cover for the catalogue to an exhibition at the Chrysler Museum in Norfolk in 1983. The location is just

even 1/400th of a second to slow or stop movement of the loco-motives and cars, rendering them in sharp detail. This required that the shutter speed of all his lenses be very accurately cali-brated, and that the electrical solenoids that tripped the shutters be adjusted to delay opening the shutters for a few milliseconds so that the flashbulbs could ignite and reach maximum intensi-ty before the shutters opened and the film was exposed. A shut-ter that was a bit fast or a solenoid that operated a bit slow could result in a uselessly underexposed negative.

The most commonly used flashbulbs were Sylvania Blue Dot No. 2's. While not the most powerful bulb available, this bulb flashed precisely and rapidly enough to permit shutter synchro-nization to a 1/400th of a second. Other, smaller bulbs, most often the No. 0 or No. 25, were also used for highlights or other special lighting. Occasionally No. 3 bulbs were used for their brute power, but they were very slow and could not be synchro-nized to the camera's shutter. They were useful if the subject was static enough to permit open flash.

From the beginning of the project until his trip of March 1956, Link used flash equipment wired in parallel. In parallel wiring, each flashbulb was wired independently. The system had the advantage of accommodating an occasional single misfire, but suffered two more serious weaknesses. The first was that there was no easy way to check for circuit continuity. Whole banks of bulbs could become disconnected from the circuit with-out indication, causing dark patches and ruining the exposure. The parallel system also took a lot of power. Photos of large areas needing lots of light sometimes required up to 12 six-volt "hot shot" batteries, each weighing about 6 pounds, to fire the bulbs.

In an effort to create a better and more responsive system, Link developed a battery-capacitor power supply with all the

a few feet from a color photograph made in the Colonna Shipyards (see page 88) and was made the same night. (NW–419A)

bulbs wired in series, like old-fashioned Christmas tree lights. The electric current to fire the bulbs had to pass through each one of them. If one connection was open or one bulb was defective, nothing would work. A surge of high voltage from small 67½ volt batteries, stored in capacitors in the power supply, replaced high current in the previous system. In an effort to help isolate problems and reduce the amount of time needed to check for discontinuities in the system, the new power supply was subdivided into three separate circuits, each of which could be continuously monitored. If one of the circuits was interrupted, a pilot light on the power supply went off—and Link walked out along the wires to find the problem. This new power supply also had another 30-volt circuit to trip the shutter solenoids of three cameras. It could fire up to sixty flashbulbs from a single switch. Link referred to the new system as "liberating," because it was lighter and supplied the information he needed to insure that his lighting would work at the critical moment.

The power supply weighed perhaps ten pounds and was carried in a small case made of red fibreboard. This was the heart of Link's flash system, never leaving the photographer's side when he was on location. The flash reflectors were another of Link's innovations. Some of them were made up of groups of standard single flash reflectors, while others, holding between four and eighteen bulbs, had been custom made of spun aluminum to Winston's specifications. Each reflector had its own telescoping stand, some of which would reach twelve feet into the air. Holding them in place was always a problem and rocks and old boards were often called into use to keep them upright if it was a breezy night. The power supply and all the reflectors were connected with stranded 14-gauge neoprene-insulated wire. Three-quarters of a mile of wire and all the reflectors, cases of bulbs,

tripods, film, and cameras fit into a small trailer that was pulled behind Link's 1952 Buick convertible.

The camera of choice for almost all of the photographs in the entire project was the Graphic View camera, a metal-bodied 4 × 5 inch view camera. The cameras were simple, light, and rugged, but the photographer always babied them, as he did all his equipment. Following a night's shooting, all the equipment had to be packed in a precise manner, no matter how late the hour, or how tired Link and his assistants might be.

Because it was difficult to calculate the precise effect of the flash lighting of the night shots, Link would try to protect himself by making at least two and preferably three negatives of each image. He would usually set up the cameras right next to each other, but might vary the individual photos by using longer or shorter focal length lenses for a more close-in or wide angle view of the scene. On occasion, he might set two cameras to make a vertical image and the third to make a horizontal one. The most frequently used black and white film was Kodak Super Panchro Press Type B, with an ASA/ISO speed of 100, which was moderately fast for the time. Color transparencies were made on Ektachrome or Anscochrome, each with a film speed of ASA/ISO 24. Ektacolor negative film was also used.

Loaded down like Mathew Brady crossing a Civil War battlefield, Link and an assistant moved out into the countryside to make this record of the last of steam railroading. In the process they would ask local people to help set up all the equipment. Some were enlisted to be in the pictures to provide the human spark found in so many of them. It was fun for Winston and his assistants, but it was hard, slow work.

LEFT AND ABOVE:

The double tanks at Buena Vista, Virginia, on the Shenandoah Division, had been constructed to permit watering two locomotives on double-headed trains simultaneously; they were an unusual landmark on the line. On this March night in 1956, Link set up one of his most ambitious multiple camera exposures here.

Three synchronized cameras using lenses of different focal lengths were used in recording a single image at the same instant.

One camera, equipped with a 3⅝ inch wide angle lens, was placed near the tracks for a powerful vertical photo (far left) that emphasizes the massiveness of the two 50,000-gallon water tanks.

(NW–853) The second camera (above) used a 5¼ inch normal lens to record the whole scene. (NW–854) The third camera equipped with a normal lens, is set at a slightly lower angle (left) to emphasize the mass of Y6 No. 2172 against the tanks. (NW–855)

The combination of a
gloomy day in January 1959,
and the mass of the A class
locomotive with its plume
of smoke enlivened by a
bed of steam, make what
might have been a very
ordinary photograph into a
romantic image of steam
power at its virile best. This
is time freight No. 84 at
Bonsack, Virginia.
(NW–1998)

Class J, No. 602 pulls Train 16, The Cavalier, out of Williamson, West Virginia, bound for Roanoke and Norfolk. Link ran backwards along the platform with his Rolleiflex as the train eased out of the station and picked up speed. At right is his contact sheet of negatives, and at far right is one of the frames he picked for enlargement. (NW–2018 to 2029)

# THUNDER ON BLUE RIDGE

Just a few miles east of downtown Roanoke, the main line of the Norfolk and Western's Norfolk Division passed up Blue Ridge, the last major climb before the long descent to Tidewater and the coal shipping docks at Norfolk and Lamberts Point. Until the N&W's merger with the Virginia Railway in 1959 offered an easier route east, all N&W traffic to the coast moved over Blue Ridge. The grade there is 8½ miles long and it is pitched at 1.2%, meaning that it rises 12 feet for every 1000 feet of length. This doesn't sound very steep, but it was a heavy challenge for a freight train because of the train's length and the great tonnage being hauled. Sometimes even two engines weren't enough.

Link made his first photographs here almost by accident. Blue Ridge was convenient to the N&W's Shaffers Crossing yards and the East Roanoke Shops, where he was making night photos. To keep busy during the day he looked around for shooting locations nearby—and found Blue Ridge. It proved to be a good spot. There were fast passenger trains, mixed freight trains working to maintain a schedule, and heavily loaded coal extras that weren't scheduled but moved across the line as the demand for coal required. The first few photos made there were so good that he concentrated his efforts at Blue Ridge for several days in December 1957 and January 1958, making both photographs and tape recordings of train sounds.

A perfect vista point for his photographs existed about three quarters of the way up the grade at a spot where a rickety bridge carried a narrow road across the tracks. If one looked west from this vantage, the tracks moved down to the west, then curved to the south, running along the northern shoulder of a broad valley that opened to the south. Looking from the other side of the bridge, the open vista changed abruptly as the double-tracked main line went into a shallow cut and the tracks quickly disappeared around a bend to the north. The bridge, subsequently removed because it was so dangerous to motorists, permitted quick passage from one side of the tracks to the other. Because the sun was to the south during the midday hours, Link could choose either to have the light on the train, if he shot from the south side of the tracks, or dramatically behind the train if he was on the other side. By late afternoon, the sun switched sides of the track, so the site offered a number of very different possibilities for lighting.

It was a busy spot and a fine place to photograph the fastest and most powerful N&W equipment under way and working hard. Many of the heavy freights offered the photographer a bonus, because an extra pusher engine was often required to get the train up the grade. The pushers were stationed at the foot of the grade at Boaz Siding, where they waited to pick up the heavily loaded eastbound coal and freight trains that required their assistance.

Link loved Boaz Siding and sometimes went there just to be next to the locomotives and spend a little time with the engine crew as they waited for trains. The spot seemed remarkably remote, considering that Roanoke was just a few miles away. A giant weeping willow sheltered the siding. A rough table and benches had been slapped together. Here the crews of the pusher engines could get out of the cabs and relax while waiting for the next train needing a push over the grade. Link made one of his most memorable photographs here: the willow droops its

LEFT: Winston Link called this expressionistic image of a locomotive moving west on the Blue Ridge grade, *Class A in a Hurry*. He emphasized speed by using a relatively slow shutter speed to capture its rolling energy. This photograph was made the same instant as the image on pages 62 and 63. (NW–2128)

branches over the massive geometry of a pusher as the engine crew sits beneath it enjoying their coffee. The photograph brought together men and machine with the softening touch of nature that the photographer so enjoyed.

Boaz Siding was later the site for several other remarkable photographs. *Highball for the Double Header*, one of only two color photos made at night, was shot at the switchman's shack a few feet east of Boaz Siding. Three other night photographs were made from this spot including the complicated *Class A, Lanterns and Funnels*, and two which included the same locomotive shot at the same instant with two cameras placed at different vantage points: *Class A in a Hurry*, and *Empty Coal Hopper Train Between Bonsack and Vinton, Virginia*. How different these two images are from Winston's first work along the line just four years before. By this time the photographer had polished his technique to the point where he could relinquish the earlier precision of his documentation in favor of a powerful expressionism: incredible energy revealed through thundering movement. *Class A in a Hurry* is particularly demonstrative of the complex motions and articulations of a steam locomotive, from the flow of smoke and steam to the reciprocating and rotating motions of the wheels and drive gear. Link deliberately used a shutter speed of only 1/200th of a second to slow but not stop the motion of the huge machine and create a blur of pure energy.

Today the great coal trains no longer pass over Blue Ridge and trees have grown up closely along the right of way. Other rail traffic continues, however, and the roadbed is as immaculate and well maintained as these photographs show it, almost forty years ago.

The photograph opposite and the one to the right are of the same locomotive, made seconds apart as the pusher rumbled under the small bridge from which Winston Link worked. (NW–1587, 1588)

FAR RIGHT: A Y6
equipped with a water car
for extra boiler water works
a freight train up the grade
on a cold day in January,
1958. (NW–1650)

RIGHT: The rear end of the
same freight is brought up
by a Y6 pusher. (NW–1651)

ON THESE PAGES AND THE TWO FOLLOWING: With one last mighty effort, Y6 pusher No. 2152 completes the job of moving a coal extra over Blue Ridge grade. Then the brakeman pulls the pin on the coupler and the train continues over the hump toward Norfolk as the pusher slows, reverses, and runs back down to Boaz Siding. (NW–1909, and 1916 to 1920)

LEFT: Moving westward between Bonsack and Vinton, Virginia, with a load of empty coal hopper cars, Class A 1226 is downbound on the Blue Ridge grade. While Link could have used a faster shutter speed, he set the shutter at 1/200th to capture the magnificent dynamics of the motion of this huge locomotive. (NW–2129)

FOLLOWING PAGES, LEFT: This photograph, which Winston Link called *Class A, Lanterns and Funnels,* was one of the last made of steam on the N&W. Setting up his camera outside one window of this little switchman's shack, Link had to make two exposures to achieve the effect he wanted. First he set the focus for the tracks outside the opposite window, then refocussed for the interior of the room, marking the camera each time. Link's first exposure was for the locomotive, which required thirty-one No. 2 flashbulbs. He then reset the camera and re-exposed the film for a brief time exposure to get the lighted kerosene lamp, followed by a single flashbulb to light the interior. Outside, Dave Plowden, Link's assistant was, in Link's words, "waving farewell to this dream of night scenes on the Norfolk and Western." (NW–2132)

FOLLOWING PAGES, RIGHT: Nowhere is Winston Link's directorial polish put to more effective use than in this image of the "Honey Hole" at Boaz Siding. Here, the engine crew have a snack under an old willow, while the caboose of the next train to be helped over the grade passes the siding on the main line before slowing to a stop. (NW–1977)

# A COLOR PORTFOLIO

Afternoon sun on corn shocks makes long shadows as train 202 nears the end of its run near Watauga, Virginia. (NW–47K)

Published here for the first time is a portfolio of color photographs that Winston Link created along the railroad during the course of his documentation of the Norfolk and Western. Color did not constitute a large part of his project, although Link would use it when it seemed particularly appropriate. Thus it's no surprise to find that many of his color photos were made along the N&W's Abingdon Branch, a pastoral setting for the twilight of steam.

Shooting color at night was extremely difficult, not only because color film is so slow and required so much light, but also because the exposure and contrast range of color transparency and color negative film are so restricted. Without precise balance and control it was all too easy to lose the middle range balance and move from underexposure to overexposure. Black and white film was much more forgiving; areas of overexposure or underexposure could be corrected in the printing process. A further problem was that Winston, who developed and printed all the black and white work in his own studio, had to send the color work to outside laboratories. It was the one part of his work over which he had no direct control, and he was always concerned that the color labs would be either insensitive to what he wanted or, worse, ruin the photographs through inattention to correct processing procedures. Both proved to be true on occasion and he was always nervous when he sent film to the color lab. To guard against accident Link never sent all the film from an assignment, whether for a commercial client or the railroad, to the lab at once. Each film holder was numbered outside and had a little plastic tab inside which printed the same number on the edge of the negative when it was exposed. Link would note the numbers of the film holders when he made the exposure so he could compare his prior calculations with the exact exposures. The numbering also made it easy to identify sheets of film that might require special processing for one reason or another. By recording the number of each film holder when he made an exposure, he could later sort out the films in his darkroom and parcel them out to the processors in two or three batches so as to avoid complete loss if one was improperly processed.

Throughout the entire project, only two night photographs were created in color, *Colonna Shipyards*, photographed in 1955, at the beginning of the documentation, and *Highball for the Double Header*, shot in 1959, one of the last night photos he made.

Winston recalls a story about *Highball for the Double Header* that tells a lot about the changing perceptions of photography and photographic documentation. Every aspect of this photograph was meticulously planned. Three cameras were used, two for color and one for black and white film. On a previous trip Link had measured off the entire site so that he could make precise lighting calculations. He also brought the two lanterns, the one in the switchman's hand and the red one in the window of the shack, back to New York so that he could experiment with the correct amount of shielding to use on the flashbulbs placed within them in order to balance their light output to match the rest of the image.

Link took such care with this photograph because he planned to use it as the cover for one of the railroad sound albums that he was planning. Shortly after the album was released Link received a letter from an admirer in California who wrote expressing his amazement at Link's good fortune that the

switchman left his red lantern on the windowsill of the shack, because it added just the right highlight to the photo. By the time this image appeared on the record cover in 1959, photographs had come to be regarded as true documents of events that seemed to happen by quirks of fate, not as the result of careful planning and precise direction.

Still, the chief reason that Link did so little color work at night (and perhaps an important reason why there were so few color photographs made during the day as well) was the nature of the subject. Link's photographs carry their narrative either through human activities or through their structure, with a strong emphasis on form, light, and space, not color. His response to questions about why so few color photos were made at night is pure Winston Link. "The train was black and white! The engine was black, smoke is white, steam is white, cars are black, track is black, night is black. What am I going to do with color?"

Autumn on the Abingdon Branch was another matter. The Abingdon Branch photographs are strong reminders of Link's deep appreciation for trees and clean water, a fundamental love of nature that his father had inculcated within him. Some of these pictures are also reminders that nineteenth-century America still existed in parts of the country as late as the middle of the twentieth century. Several of Link's images could be modern transliterations of paintings by George Inness or chromolithographs by Currier and Ives. A century seems to fall away unnoticed, as farmers stack the corn stalks and shuck the ears in the fields, while a horse-drawn wagon waits nearby and the Virginia Creeper meanders along in the background. Link was unacquainted with the history of American painting, but he collected Currier and Ives prints with railroad subject matter. None of the Currier and Ives lithographs in his collection resembles the photographs in this book, but it is worth noting how easily that imagery comes to mind when the subject matter was still vital, as it was along the Abingdon Branch in 1955.

Engine 382 reduces smoke
as the Virginia Creeper near
Lansing passes a line of
freshly laundered clothes.
(NW–76K)

Pungent coal smoke lifts
sufficiently to show train
201 as it makes its way
past a point that Winston
Link called "overlook,"
between Damascus and
Creek Junction. This was a
typical "consist," four to
eight freight cars, an
ancient mail and baggage
car, and an equally old
passenger car, painted in
the Norfolk and Western's
famous Tuscan red.
(NW–61K)

Throttle closed and safety valve popping, Engine 382 pulling Train 201 southbound, comes to a stop at the water tank at Creek Junction, named for White Top Laurel Creek, visible to the left. The train will also drop off mail here for Konnerock and other tiny hamlets nearby. It may also take on water as it has been working up a 2.2% grade for fifteen miles. The grade will increase to nearly 3% before reaching White Top, nine miles south. (NW-20K)

OPPOSITE: A few townspeople watch from the front of the general store and post office as Train 202 slows on the 2.5% grade to White Top and pulls into Nella, North Carolina.

The railroad called the tiny station Nella, but the United States Post Office regarded the hamlet as Husk. This is the home of Jimbo, a dog whose "singing" would accompany engineer

Nichols's custom whistle as engine 382 rolled through town twice a day six days a week. (NW–75K)

Stopping at Creek Junction for a photograph and to take on water, the southbound Virginia Creeper's Engine 382 lifts its safety valve while engineer Joe McNew and brakeman J. M. "Skutch" Stevens pose for the camera on the bank of White Top Laurel Creek. (NW–64K)

LEFT: Two friendly pigs ignore Train 202 as it rumbles across Horse Creek in Tuckerdale, North Carolina. Today the metal-roofed house remains and the church in the background has expanded, but all traces of the railroad have vanished. (NW–133K)

OPPOSITE: Town, road, railroad, and river all share a shallow valley as Train 201 pulls out of Lansing, North Carolina, and crosses Big Horsepen Creek, a few miles north of West Jefferson. (NW–68K)

LEFT: Morning light highlights the southbound Virginia Creeper crossing bridge 52, the highest bridge on the Abingdon Branch, just south of Creek Junction. (NW–136K)

OPPOSITE: South of Nella/Husk, North Carolina, the Abingdon Branch followed Horse Creek and Big Horsespen Creek, frequently moving from one side to the other. Here double-headed Train 201 sounds a crossing signal as the locomotives roll across bridge 79 on the way to West Jefferson.

This image is a favorite of the photographer's because it shows so well the abrupt mechanical intrusion of the train in a bucolic landscape. (NW–44K)

RIGHT: Leaving Damascus, Virginia, Train 201 passes a splendid old maple as the train enters more rugged country on the way to White Top, the highest point in the eastern United States served by scheduled railroad passenger service. (NW–36K)

OPPOSITE: When Winston Link began documenting the Abingdon Branch, Engine 382 still had its headlight mounted high up on the smoke box, in the old-fashioned way, and he regarded it as "the prettiest engine on the Abingdon Branch." Here 382, working hard, brings Train 202 across bridge 8, just a few miles short of Abingdon. (NW–137K)

RIGHT: The Powhatan
Arrow to Cincinnati moves
smartly across the
magnificent bridge west of
Cooper Tunnel. This was the
N&W's best passenger train;
it ran the entire east-west
stretch of the railroad's
main line from Norfolk to
Cincinnati. On this warm
afternoon in 1955, traffic is
light and J class 604
handles the train with little
effort. With his low camera
angle, Link emphasized the
strength of the bridge as
well as the sleek polish of
the train. (NW–5K)

The Pocahontas on its way
from Cincinnati to Norfolk
takes the Blue Ridge grade
at speed in early January,
1958. (NW–34C)

Empty coal boppers roll westbound after passing through Montgomery Tunnel. The round sign is a speed warning to eastbound trains coming downgrade and about to enter the west portal of the tunnel. (NW–121K)

OPPOSITE:

In a scene that could have been pictured in a Currier and Ives chromolithograph a century ago, workers toss feed corn into a wagon in a field near Watauga, Virginia as the southbound Virginia Creeper passes. (NW–34K)

RIGHT:

Class J Engine 607, westbound from Norfolk, has crossed the bridge over the Elizabeth River and passes a drydocked tug undergoing a refit in the Colonna Shipyards. The N&W met Tidewater at Norfolk, which explains the juxtaposition of water and rail. This photograph, made in September 1955, was the first of only two night shots Link ever made in color. The film was so slow that the exposure required the use of No. 3 flash bulbs, which were very powerful, but too slow to be synchronized to the camera's shutter. To make the exposure the shutter was opened, the bulbs were fired, and the shutter was quickly closed. (NW–10K)

OPPOSITE:

Winston Link called the second night photo of the

N&W he made in color *Highball for the Double Header,* and used it as the cover of a record album of sounds of the railroad. The photograph was planned for months: three cameras recorded the exposure, for which there was no second chance. Made at 3:40 a.m. on April 23, 1959, it required thirty-two No. 2 flashbulbs for general illumination and three No. 25 flashbulbs to light the interior of the switchman's shack and the two lanterns. Link has described the scene as "steam railroading at its zenith," and it was one of the last photographs made of steam power on the Norfolk and Western Railway. (NW–32K)

Two A Class locomotives, with a water car between them, pull a long mixed freight up Blue Ridge grade, their smoke and steam exhaust drifting off toward the darkening eastern sky. (NW–26C)

OPPOSITE:

A double header coal freight with two Y6 engines works so hard on the Blue Ridge grade that the locomotives are all but hidden by their own smoke and steam exhaust on a cold day in January, 1958. (NW–38C)

# A DAY ON THE ABINGDON BRANCH

The morning train—eight or ten freight cars, a baggage-mail-express car, and a passenger car—loops past the Lutheran Church in Damascus. (NW–642)

It wasn't long after he arrived in Roanoke in the spring of 1955 to start his record of the railroad that Ben Dulaney told Winston about the N&W's Abingdon Branch. Link knew nothing of it before that time and now says that "I went to Abingdon because Ben Dulaney sent me there. He said, 'You've got to go ride that Abingdon Branch before you do anything else. It's so good!' And he was right."

The Abingdon Branch had been independent at one time. It was begun in the late nineteenth century as a series of speculative mineral and logging railroads. Acquired by the N&W in 1919, it extended at one time for more than seventy-five miles from Abingdon, Virginia, to Elkland (now Todd), North Carolina. But the lumber ran out, and by the mid-thirties the railroad operated only as far as West Jefferson, North Carolina, a bit more than fifty-five rail miles south of Abingdon.

The Abingdon Branch was a very high-maintenance operation: the N&W ran it with increasing reluctance. Passenger service was finally dropped in 1963 and the entire branch was abandoned in 1977. Fortunately the United States Forest Service and other public and private interests purchased the right of way in Virginia from Abingdon to the North Carolina border and have maintained the right of way and the bridges as the "Virginia Creeper Trail" for hikers and bicyclers.

Starting in Abingdon, a stately old town located in the southwest wedge of Virginia just a few miles from the Tennessee border, the rails moved south across the rolling fields of small farms, past the hamlets of Watauga and Alvarado to Damascus. Just north of Damascus, the largest town on the branch other than Abingdon itself, the grade begins to climb, and after leaving Damascus the country changes dramatically. The railroad entered country marked by sharp slopes covered with second-growth timber and deep valleys, many of them with small streams meandering through them. Working along the creeks, the railroad climbed steadily toward White Top Gap. Moving south, the land use changed as the topography dictated, from small farms to much more isolated mountain cabins. South of White Top the land is too steep to farm practically, and what agriculture exists there is strictly for subsistence, a cow or two, a few chickens and hogs raised for family consumption. The roads are difficult and slow, particularly between Damascus and Tuckerdale. From Tuckerdale to West Jefferson the country opens up a bit. The terminal point of the Abingdon Branch was West Jefferson, North Carolina, one of the larger towns in the area, although its population when Winston Link photographed it was less than 1,000 people.

The branch was rugged railroading. Almost 110 trestles and bridges, most built of local timber, carried the rails across depressions and streams. The grade approaching White Top, at more than 3,500 feet the highest point ever reached by regularly scheduled passenger trains east of the Rockies, ran for miles at an average of 2.2 to 2.5%, and touched 3% in the two miles before reaching the station. At one time as many as seven trains a day, including two round-trip passenger trains, ran over the line, but by 1955 service had long since been reduced to a single mixed train. Consisting of a few freight cars, an antique baggage car, and an equally venerable passenger coach, the train (numbered 201 southbound and 202 northbound) made the run every day except Sunday. Decades earlier the train had been aptly

nicknamed the "Virginia Creeper," because its maximum speed was 25 miles per hour; between Taylors Valley and Nella an 18-mile an-hour speed limit was required. In fact the train rarely ran even that fast, and about the only thing that was certain in the schedule was its 7:30 A.M. departure time from Abingdon. Officially it was due into West Jefferson at 11:15 A.M. and back in Abingdon at 3:10 P.M., but the needs of freight haulers took precedence over the passenger schedule and the train might well arrive home hours late.

If anything marked the Abingdon Branch other than the magnificent mountain beauty of the country through which it ran, it was age. Everything about the railroad's equipment was old, a warp that twisted time the moment one boarded the train in Abingdon. The Class M, 4–8–0 locomotives, nicknamed "Mollies," which powered the Abingdon Branch trains, were about fifty years old, and the stations were of equal vintage or earlier. The passenger and baggage/mail/express cars also dated from the same period and were heated with coal stoves. Yet the operation was so complete in its antiquity that one felt that this was just as it should be and that the train perfectly matched the country and towns through which it passed.

Changes, when they had occurred, had simply been added to what existed, so the whole system was the visible result of design by accident, built through decades of accretion. On buildings along the right of way, new signs were tacked up next to or covering old ones and about the only things that seemed to change in the stations were the pictorial calendars from local businesses—and sometimes even they didn't change very fast. A month or two, even a year or two, might slip by before the calendar was changed.

Link came to Abingdon in mid-June 1955 to make his first trips on the Virginia Creeper. Those trips, Friday, June 17 and Saturday, June 18, 1955, resulted in more than 200 daylight photographs, all made with a Rolleiflex, a hand-held camera producing an image 2¼ inches square. With one exception the photographs were made from either inside the train or alongside it during station stops.

Link recalls that this first trip was to be a relaxed event. "I went to look at the Abingdon Branch. I was only making a record of the trip. I didn't think I was making a permanent record of the railroad. I was just shooting what I could easily get and not knocking myself out. Now, of course I made a lot of pictures. I made pictures of people riding the train and pictures from the train. When the train went around a curve you could photograph it all, including the engine, from the Dutch door on the last car."

It is this first group of photos that forms the central structure

| | FIRST CLASS 201 Mixed Lv. Daily Ex. Sunday | Time Table No. 10 EFFECTIVE Sunday, April 29, 1956 STATIONS | FIRST CLASS 202 Mixed Ar. Daily Ex. Sunday | Telephone Calls | Siding Capacity in Feet |
|---|---|---|---|---|---|
| | A. M. | | P. M. | | |
| .00 | 7.30 | Abingdon....................w | 3.10 | — — ··· ·· | Yard |
| .38 | ......... | Yard | ......... | | 1138 |
| 4.31 | ......... | Watauga | f........ | | 400 |
| 9.06 | f 7.55 | Alvarado | f 2.41 | | 460 |
| 10.90 | f......... | Delmar | f......... | | ..... |
| 12.51 | f......... | Drowning Ford | f......... | | ..... |
| 14.52 | f......... | Vails Mill | f......... | | ..... |
| 16.04 | s 8.20 | Damascus | s 2.16 | —.— | 820 |
| 17.82 | f 8.25 | Laureldale | f 2.06 | | 400 |
| 22.77 | f 8.40 | Taylors Valley | f 1.51 | —. .... | 1605 |
| 26.57 | f 8.58 | Creek Junction...............w | f 1.36 | | 1120 |
| 30.60 | f 9.19 | Green Cove | f 1.21 | —. —.— | 390 |
| 33.53 | f 9.54 | Whitetop | f 1.06 | —... — | 990 |
| 39.53 | f 10.16 | Nella | f 12.41 | | 280 |
| 43.04 | f 10.29 | Tuckerdale..................w | f 12.29 | —.— — | 480 |
| 46.50 | f 10.39 | Lansing | f 12.19 | —.... | 804 |
| 47.82 | f 10.44 | Bina | f 12.09 | | ..... |
| 49.98 | f 10.51 | Warrensville | f 12.01PM | —.... | 390 |
| 52.95 | f 11.01 | Smethport | f 11.51 | | 451 |
| 55.45 | s 11.15 | West Jefferson............w Y s | 11.45 | —. .. — | 1600 |
| | A. M. | | A. M. | | |

No. 201 has right over No. 202 to West Jefferson.
Regular trains between Abingdon and West Jefferson are not required to observe Rule No. 99.
EXTRA trains must run expecting to find regular trains unprotected between these stations.
MAIN LINE DERAILS—Main Line Derails are located as follows:
Damascus, between station and junction switch.
Whitetop, 300 feet south of passing siding switch. (Spring switch derail)
West Jefferson, Mile Post 55 plus 576 feet. (Spring switch derail)

Abingdon Branch trains will reduce speed to five (5) miles per hour before passing over road crossings at the following locations:
Mile Post 47 plus 5,000 feet.
Mile Post 50 plus 3,700 feet.
Mile Post 52 plus 1,590 feet.
Mile Post 53 plus 4,750 feet.

OPPOSITE:

Morning Train 201 southbound passes the freight station at Abingdon. Both freight and passenger stations exist today. (NW–1199)

At left is a timetable of the Abingdon branch preserved by the photographer.

ABOVE: Twice a day—
except Sunday—the little
Alvarado station and Post
Office was a busy spot as
the Virginia Creeper came
through. (NW-205)

RIGHT: The station is
gone now and the grocery
store is vacant, but the
church remains in Alvarado,
a few miles south of
Abingdon. The morning train
has stopped to handle the
mail, set off a freight car,
and pick up passengers.
(NW-639)

96

RIGHT AND OPPOSITE:

W. P. Cole, brakeman, moves a gondola along an adjacent siding by the use of a pole, which fitted into concave indentations on the locomotive and freight car frames. When not in use the pole was carried on hangers under the tender. Cars could be easily moved in this manner without requiring the locomotive to switch tracks, but "polin' the gon" was a dangerous practice that has long been prohibited.

(NW–220, 223)

of this chapter, a typical day aboard and alongside Trains 201 and 202 of the Abingdon Branch. Link was to return to the Abingdon Branch at least three more times, including a two-week stay in the fall of 1957, just a few weeks before the line was dieselized. Photographs are included from all these trips. They fill out the experience of riding the train and enjoying the Virginia Creeper as it slowly passed by.

I accompanied Winston Link on that final trip and can attest to his observation that "coming down to work on the railroad photos was not a vacation. It was hard work!" On his previous visits, Winston had staked out a number of sites where he wanted to make photographs. Getting to many of them was another matter. The roads, particularly south of Damascus, often followed old logging road rights of way and were treacherous and winding as they ascended and descended the shoulders of White Top Mountain. The 4 × 5 cameras were screwed to their tripods and

placed on the platform that had long since replaced the back seat of Link's Buick convertible, ready to be pulled out the moment we stopped. If we were lucky, we could get the large cameras in place, make the exposures and dash to the next location twice in the distance between Abingdon and West Jefferson. When the train was on its return run northbound, we could make only one 4 × 5 photo between the two towns as the train was traveling downgrade and moving faster, except for slowing for a sharp upgrade from Lansing to White Top. Thus a whole day might be spent in making only three or four photographs.

Yet the experience was exhilarating. Winston said that "it was like a hunting party. Not hunting for a wild animal but hunting for the engine, looking for it to appear suddenly because it went through such rugged country. You would see it one moment and the next it would disappear behind a mountain and you couldn't find it until all of a sudden it would pop up somewhere else. The only way you could find it easily was to ride the train. While it was a wonderful experience to ride the train, it was also a pleasure to go back and find the locations. There was a lot of discovery involved with the whole thing. You would run into those old stores with their old equipment, old scales and show cases, and it would all seem so natural."

Looking at his photographs of the people gathered at the stations Link remembered that "the train's coming in was a big event. People would come down to see if there was any mail for them, or just come down to see the train and see their friends who would have come down for the same reason. Sometimes this was the biggest event of the day." The train helped to stitch the towns together, maintaining contact between the villages in these deep valleys.

Since the train was such an event in the lives of these moun-

tain folks, Link devoted more time to photographing people on the Abingdon Branch than anywhere else along the line. There were the men of the train crew, the townspeople, mailmen, passengers and their friends, kids down along the tracks waiting for a handout of lollipops from the conductor, and passersby who just stop to watch the train. Farmers who saw the train almost daily went about their business with hardly a look at the machine passing them by—and the photographer liked that.

The quality of the railroad in this countryside was a profoundly poetic experience for Link, and his description of the trains of the Abingdon Branch is couched with wonder and deep appreciation: "The locomotives at times are almost incidental to the picture. They add to the rural scenery: streams, little bridges and country roads, trees, mountains, cows. They would come by, then be gone with just a little whiff of coal smoke."

RIGHT: Bridge 42 south
of Damascus, southbound.
Winston Link made the
photograph from the
passenger car, hanging over
the Dutch door as the train
rounded a curve and
crossed the small timber
bridge. (NW–228)

OPPOSITE: Smoke from
doubleheaded Train 201
lifts to show the
southbound train passing
through a sweeping S curve
at "overlook," a name
Winston Link gave to a
point on the way to Creek
Junction where the tracks
passed below the winding
road to White Top.
(NW–1291)

LEFT: Train 201 and the mail truck leave Creek Junction together, as Engine 429 works up the grade to bridge 52 crossing White Top Laurel Creek. (NW–233)

OPPOSITE: Locomotive 382, pulling Train 201 to White Top, leaves Green Cove station. The trees are gone now, but the Buchanan family home and the station itself remain much as they were in October, 1956. (NW–1236)

RIGHT:

W. M. Buchanan was station agent at Green Cove, Virginia, from 1912 to 1938. When Link photographed him, he was manager of the Western Union office, postmaster, and operator of a small store in the station, which he and his family bought from the railroad. He was more interested in the pictures on the calendars than the dates. (NW–1245)

OPPOSITE:

W. M. Buchanan prepares a grocery order as folks from nearby wait patiently at the station for the arrival of the Virginia Creeper. On the left side, W. R. Farmer, Vinton Green, "Sandy" the dog, and Eleanor Buchanan chat with Carver Walls, Leslie Greer, Mrs. Fay Luther, Brenda Luther, Janet Farmer (obscured) and Bolena Greer. Unlike so many other stations that the railroad demolished when passenger service was terminated, Green Cove remains today because it was owned by the Buchanan family. Subsequently it was acquired by the National Forest Service and has been restored to the appearance seen here. The stove, shelves, counters, scale, and glass display cases are still in place. (NW–1248)

LEFT: Engine 382, all but hidden by wood waiting to be loaded into flat cars, brings Train 201 southbound into White Top station, at the highest point on the run. From here it is down grade to West Jefferson. (NW–1279)

ABOVE LEFT: Conductor Ralph "Candy Man" White hands the newspaper to Gladys Harriger. (NW–144)

ABOVE RIGHT: Mrs. Gladys Harriger, station agent at White Top, Virginia (and one of only four women agents on the N&W at the time), works on a quilt while waiting for the train. White Top was distinguished by being the highest point (3,577 feet) east of the Rockies reached by a regularly scheduled passenger train. Everything about the station was old, from the broken typewriter to unused signal lamps— night trains had not run on the Abingdon Branch for years. Mrs. Harriger has made good use of old telegraph pole insulators by putting them on the legs of her chair to make it easier to move. (NW–660)

ABOVE:

At West Jefferson,

North Carolina, engines

were turned on a "wye,"

a short Y-shaped junction

of track and a siding.

(NW–150)

FAR RIGHT:

Children stand transfixed as

Train 201 pulls into Nella.

This tiny North Carolina

town had two names: to the

railroad it was Nella, but the

U. S. Post Office knew it as

Husk. Nella was supposedly

named after Allen, a

railroad man. As there was

already another town of

Allen on the railroad, the

station name was simply

reversed. (NW–149)

The sunlight of a late fall afternoon in 1956 touches Train 202 just north of West Jefferson. The rugged hills of Ashe County, North Carolina serve as a massive backdrop as the small train wends its way through the beautiful country that marked so much of its journey. (NW–1259)

Joe McNew was one of the two principal engineers of the Abingdon Branch in its last years. McNew was famous for hard driving, getting every pound of tractive effort from the aged M class locomotives. (NW–215)

FAR LEFT: Engineer Joe
McNew leans out of the
cab to maneuver 429's
tender under the spout of
the water tank at West
Jefferson, North Carolina.
(NW–152)

LEFT: Fireman
D. S. Nichols stands on
the water spout as 429
tales takes on water in
West Jefferson.
(NW–156)

LEFT: Engineer Joe McNew passes his money to Jerry Witherspoon for his weekly copy of *Grit* as Engine 429 waits in West Jefferson for the return trip to Abingdon. (NW–256)

ABOVE: Earl Carper, the Virginia Creeper's baggage and package freight man, unloads a box shipped via Railway Express at West Jefferson. Rail shipment was the most common way to send even small packages to this area in 1955. (NW–254)

ABOVE: Fireman D. S. Nichols, his left foot on the air valve that opens the butterfly doors to the firebox, shovels coal as Engine 429 prepares to pull Train 202 on the northbound trip from West Jefferson to Abingdon. These old locomotives had no mechanical stokers and from West Jefferson to White Top Nichols would shovel almost continuously, particularly on the thirteen-mile stretch from Lansing to White Top. From there to Abingdon his trip will be easier as the grade heads down. (NW–290)

Train 202 arrives in Lansing, a few miles north of West Jefferson, on the way back to Abingdon. The town's main street is to the left and Big Horsepen Creek is out of sight to the right. A brick fire station now occupies the station site. (NW–1253)

RIGHT, BELOW:

Some last minute mail is quickly passed aboard Train 202 as the Virginia Creeper begins to move out of Lansing. (NW–1255)

FAR RIGHT:

On October 22, 1956, Joe Dollar waits patiently as Engine 382, whistle blowing and bell ringing, crosses the road near Warrenville, North Carolina, on the return trip from West Jefferson. (NW–1252)

Ralph "Candy Man" White shows why he was the most popular railroad man on the Abingdon Branch. Every Saturday, White distributed free lollipops to the children along the line. Here he hands them out during train 202's northbound stop at Green Cove. (NW–235)

ABOVE: Train 202 was scheduled to arrive at White Top northbound at 1:06 P.M. but often arrived hours late. Whenever it did arrive, Charlie Dolinger, White Top's mailman, was waiting with the day's mail. (NW–272)

RIGHT: The southbound train was due into Lansing at 10:39 A.M., but usually arrived later. A Lansing café would put lunch for some of the train crew aboard the southbound train and this young woman, her hair put up for an evening's fun, perhaps, picked up the money and dirty dishes from the baggage car when the train came back north in the early afternoon. (NW–166)

RIGHT:

Brakeman J. M. "Skutch" Stevens demonstrates how the single passenger car was warmed. This was a mixed train, and no steam heating line connected the passenger car to the locomotive. Heat was supplied by coal shoveled into a heavy stove bolted to the car floor. (NW–246)

FAR RIGHT:

Stevens dozes in the passenger car as the train makes its return to Abingdon. (NW–170)

ABOVE:

Brakeman Stevens chats with a passenger as the Virginia Creeper makes its way north toward Abingdon. When Winston Link traveled the line there was an informal camaraderie in the single passenger car of this train and many of the passengers seemed to have known one another and the train crew for years. (NW–198)

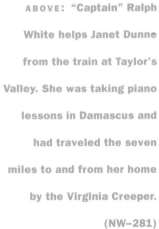

ABOVE: "Captain" Ralph White helps Janet Dunne from the train at Taylor's Valley. She was taking piano lessons in Damascus and had traveled the seven miles to and from her home by the Virginia Creeper. (NW–281)

ABOVE: Although it was Link's first visit to the Abingdon Branch, the N&W gave him full cooperation, including dropping him off at the northern end of bridge 52 at Creek Junction, the highest bridge on the Abingdon Branch, so that he could make this photograph. (NW–181)

RIGHT: It has been a long day and Train 202 is late as it crosses bridge 7 near Watauga, a few miles from Abingdon. (NW–1264)

The day's run to West Jefferson and back is finished, and Engine 429 waits at the Bristol station to pull Train 202 into the yards, as westbound Train 45, The Tennessean, thunders past on the main line. (NW–293)

With Winston Link riding on top of the cab, Train 202 waits at Abingdon to enter the main line for its return to the Abingdon station and then on to the Bristol yard. A mixed freight powered by a massive Y6, its engineer and fireman waving to the ancient Mollie, heads eastward. (NW–292)

At the end of a hard day's run in the fall of 1956, Engine 382 waits on the turntable at Bristol, Virginia, while 429, its companion locomotive, takes on coal and water. The steam exhaust from their turbine generators and safety valves all but blot out an eastbound freight on the mainline in the background. Link recalls that this was a favorite spot from which to photograph, but he had many problems trying to keep his lighting circuits intact as there was so much activity at this small roundhouse. At times the turntable and engines would catch wires or cut them under the locomotives' wheels. He was working there alone on the night this photograph was made and had run the wires from the power supply on the roof of the roundhouse under the turntable to the lamps that lighted the turntable and tracks in the middle distance and background. The revolving turntable snagged the wires and pulled down all the lights, requiring everything to be set up again. It was one of his longest nights in the field. (NW–1374)

130

# WINSTON LINK: A NOTE ON HIS LIFE

Ogle Winston Link was born December 16, 1914 in Brooklyn, New York, the second child and first son of Earnest Albert Link and Ann Winston Jones Link. A sister, Eleanor, was two years older. Two more children followed Winston, a daughter several years younger who died in infancy, and Albert Link, Jr., ten years younger, who, like his father, was called Al.

Ogle and Winston were two proud names on the maternal side of the family. Both Alexander Ogle and John Winston Jones served in the United States House of Representatives in the mid-nineteenth century; Jones was Speaker of the House during the 28th Congress. With the exception of his four years at Brooklyn Polytechnic Institute, Winston Link has never used his first name, and if he bore two distinguished names from his mother's side of the family, it was his father who insisted that they be assembled so that they spelled OWL. It is a mark of his father's wry wit (which was to have such a great influence on his son), and is an acronym Winston has proudly used as a trademark.

Both parents were from the south, Ann from Virginia and Albert from West Virginia. Albert came to the New York area in the early part of the century, sometime before his marriage, to study law. But he failed the New Jersey bar examination and never took it again because, as Winston now says, "he had no one to encourage him." Instead he became a manual arts teacher, teaching woodworking courses in an elementary school in Brooklyn. While the elder Link never expressed regret at not being a lawyer, he pressed his children to train for demanding professional careers. Winston recalls that "my father made my sister become a lawyer." She was one of the first women lawyers to graduate from Brooklyn Law School and "she suffered a lot,

having to put up with the guys in her class," although law proved to be a good match for her talents and she practiced successfully for decades.

When Winston was about one year old his family moved to a nineteenth-century town house at 483 Eighth Street in Brooklyn's Park Slope neighborhood, near Prospect Park, which was to remain a family residence for almost seventy years. It was a solid middle class neighborhood, filled with children. Winston recalls his youth with great happiness and still maintains friendships with people he knew there as a child. Although he was a demanding and precise man, Albert Link was also an equally effective teacher, and Winston was an apt student. The senior Link had learned woodworking from his older brothers while growing up in rural West Virginia and passed on the information to his son. His father taught Winston meticulously how to work with wood and how to handle and use tools. To this day, Link likes nothing better than solving technical problems that require both intellectual and manual resolution. This is the stuff of high drama for him and he can turn the description of repairs on his Model A Ford or antique railroad car into fascinating stories. His father helped him there, too, for Albert was a great storyteller, and as is often the case with such people, nothing was ever boring—if it could be turned into a story.

The senior Link wished his son to have a wide variety of experiences, to look at life from a number of different vantage points. As Winston now describes it, "my father introduced me to all kinds of things to see what might take hold." One of the things to which he was introduced early on was photography. While he had to photograph with borrowed equipment, starting with his

father's 3¼ × 5½ inch Autographic Kodak, by the time Link was in high school he was so interested in the medium that he had built his own enlarger. His father took him on trips to see the sights around the city, including battleships visiting New York harbor and ceremonial overflights of airplanes, all of which he photographed. In the early thirties one of the places he and his father visited was a depression shanty town, "Hoover City," which

had sprung up in the Red Hook section of Brooklyn. A number of these humble buildings were constructed of large blocks of stone scavenged from dump sites nearby. Winston photographed here too, but "I didn't get pictures of the residents' faces. I didn't want to invade their privacy in any way." It was also about this time that Winston and several teenage friends on the block who were interested in trains began to make independent excursions

The Blue Comet, photographed in Jersey City, across from downtown Manhattan, in 1933.

In early 1939 Winston
Link's national fraternity
magazine reproduced some
of the photographs he had
shot during his first year
as a public relations
photographer.

to see these exciting machines more closely; Winston always brought his father's camera along.

He fondly recalls that "we would take the subway to the west side of Manhattan, buy a frankfurter for five cents, and take the ferry across the Hudson River to the Jersey Central or Baltimore & Ohio yards in Jersey City and Hoboken and just hang out." Sometimes Winston and his friends would go to the Jersey Central's beautiful Communipaw Station, which still rises like a Gothic vision on a low spit of land just north of Ellis Island. They went to see the line's crack Blue Comet, preparing to leave for its three-hour run to Atlantic City. "The whole train was blue," Link

remembers, "not an ugly blue but a beautiful blue. The engine, which waited way out in the yards until just before train time, as blue too, except for the smoke box which was painted a dull black. It even had nickel-plated connecting rods and running gear. It was a perfect steam engine." The earliest photo Link can recall making shows two young friends, overdressed by modern standards, posed on the front end of an Erie locomotive.

Link attended Manual Training High School in Brooklyn, which, despite its name, offered strong academic courses. It was particularly well equipped to teach sophisticated metal and woodworking techniques, courses that have all but disappeared from American secondary education. Responding to his father's urging, Link took subjects that pointed the way to a career in engineering. "My father indoctrinated me with the idea that I was going to be an engineer," and so he studied math and science. He was a good student and did well in humanities courses too, even without much work. He played on the school's hockey team, and re-calls having to get up at 3:00 A.M. and ride the trolley across town to practice at Brooklyn's Ice Palace before going on to school.

In 1933, following his father's "indoctrination," Winston enrolled at the Polytechnic Institute of Brooklyn (now Polytechnic University, but universally known as Brooklyn Poly). He received a scholarship to study civil engineering. He was a popular student and a good one academically, but was far from being an engineering "grind." He was president of his class all four years, and was elected to Tau Beta Pi, the honorary engineering society, in his junior year. Yet another talent, quite unlike engineering, was beginning to emerge. It was to become a major, if subliminal, force in his life and work. Enthralled perhaps by his father's stories, Winston Link became an unconscious actor and dramatist. This talent, which was to so influence his photographic work, appeared first at Brooklyn Poly in his fascination with language. He began by altering English to create spoonerisms of his own invention, a passion which continues to this day. (When Winston needs

money he will "chash a heck," warm himself in the winter with a cup of "choc hotlet," cool off in the summer with a dip in a "pimming swool," think about ideas by pacing "fack and borth," and fix a dead battery with a "chattery barger.") He developed remarkable abilities as a mimic, and listening to (and sometimes imitating) peculiarities of speech has also remained a lifelong fascination.

Link enjoyed creating humorous pranks as well, unknowingly preparing himself for the time when he would have to think up crazy photographic stunts for his clients. One of his favorites was what he remembers as the "hicks eating pie" routine. On several occasions while at Brooklyn Poly, Winston and a friend went to the Horn and Hardart Automat on Times Square. They each bought a piece of cherry pie and sat at a window table facing Broadway. Carefully they removed their jackets, loosened their ties, unbuttoned their vests, tucked their napkins under their chins like bibs, and proceeded to eat the pie with their hands. The scene was boldly acted, and mesmerized pedestrians watching the scene so clogged the sidewalk that the police had to be called to move them along before the pie was finished and the dumb show ended.

Winston has summarized his social career at Brooklyn Poly in a word. "I was a clown," he now laughs. The college event which was to have the greatest influence on his life was a clown-ish one. One of his most hilarious routines was a precise imitation of the instructor who taught the mechanics of materials classes. Link was particularly adept at rendering the professor's lecture on "The Red Brick." In fact, his imitation became so well known and his inattention to the subject so marked that he flunked the class, costing him his scholarship in the process. He later took the class again and passed easily.

Link graduated from Brooklyn Poly in 1937, not a good year for the country—and certainly not a good one for beginning civil engineers. Toward the end of the academic year, the staff of the school newspa-per held its annual banquet. Win-ston was the photo editor of the paper and one of its photographers. A short time before the banquet, he had gone with a reporter to Brook-lyn's Star Theatre to interview and photograph a reigning burlesque queen for an article. At the banquet, Winston gave a talk in which he imi-tated the mechanics of materials professor. He delivered the talk as though the professor had interviewed the burlesque dancer and was reporting on the event—in his best "red brick" style. It brought down the house. One of the guests was so impressed that he asked Winston to give him a call the next day. The banquet visitor was George Hammond, an executive with Carl Byoir and Associates, one of the country's largest public relations firms. Byoir had huge accounts with some of the country's largest com-

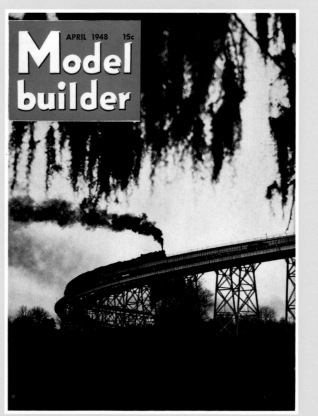

panies, B. F. Goodrich, Libby–Owens–Ford Glass and A & P among them. They needed a photographer, and George Ham-mond asked if Winston might be interested in the job. It was a long way from civil engineering, but almost the only jobs to be had for young civil engineers at the time were positions working in muddy subway excavations. Brooklyn Poly's alumni secretary urged him to take the photography job, "even if it's just for the summer," and he did. He liked it so much that he stayed five years.

Public relations is something of a game. The idea behind it is to gain credibility for your clients' products or services through favorable men-tion in news articles in newspapers and magazines without having to pay for it. In that pre-television era it was the print media that carried the day and most PR men were ex-newspaper reporters. The use of photography for publicity purposes was on the rise and Byoir decided that it needed to provide photos to complete its package of client ser-vices. It wanted pictures with "snap" and "punch" to catch the eyes of the jaded picture editors of America's newspapers and magazines. If Winston Link could put as much punch into his photos as into his after-dinner stories, he was their man.

Link was on his own. He had never studied photography, and had little photographic experience other than taking pictures for pleasure, the student newspaper work, making photos of student engineering projects at Brooklyn Poly for a little pocket money,

and shooting a few weddings. Byoir had never before had a photographer on staff and the firm was so unprepared that Link had to borrow a camera from his old school until his new employer could buy cameras and equip a proper darkroom. But the job proved to be a wonderful training ground for him. It clearly defined a point of view and developed working methods that were to shape his entire career.

First of all, photographs made for PR had to be instruction-al and informational. They had to tell a story, no matter how far-fetched it might seem, and they had to have visual excitement and drama. They just had to catch the eye. These photos were very thoroughly constructed and directed, even though they were often carefully tailored to look "candid." Of course the picture editors knew what was going on, and if a photograph was too blatant in its sales pitch it wouldn't be run. On the other hand, cleverness went a long way to overcoming their resistance to a picture's commercial intent.

One example of the oblique way that Byoir worked for its clients is seen in a photograph of a pig in a bulletproof vest illustrated in the montage of his first year's work reproduced on page 134. B. F. Goodrich Company was one of Byoir's major clients. Goodrich had commissioned tests by the Pittsburgh Testing Laboratory, an industrial and commercial product testing concern, which determined that a certain line of Goodrich tires were the best tires of their type made in the country. Byoir set out to exploit this fact by publicizing the Pittsburgh Testing Laboratory, emphasizing the care and effort they put into product testing as a way of giving credibility to the test results. Winston was sent to Pittsburgh to document the lab's activities. This turned out to be not very interesting visually. Then Link discovered that one of the laboratory's clients made bulletproof vests, which were tested by strapping a square of the bulletproof material to a pig and shooting at it. This was a perfect foil for him. Winston sent for a complete bulletproof vest, went to a local stockyards, found a pig of the right size, dressed it in the bulletproof vest, sat the nonplussed animal in a chair, and had a model hold an unloaded gun to its chest. The picture was widely reproduced.

Perhaps Link's most famous picture created for Byoir was made for the Libby–Owens–Ford account. L–O–F had just introduced "Tuf-flex" glass, a super-strong glazing product. They wanted the general public to know about it. For this job Link created what became known as the "What Is This Girl Selling?" photo. The shot shows a young woman in a bathing suit insouciantly standing on a stack of 300-pound blocks of ice, while using a small mirror to adjust her hairdo. The first tier of ice forms the legs of a table which supports the rest of the ice, and a fire rages beneath the table. Of course the product being sold was

"Tuf-flex" glass, which forms the barely visible table top. The shoot demanded not only a catchy idea, but some technical expertise as well. The ice and glass did not cooperate and kept sliding around; Link solved the problem by placing pieces of cloth between all the slabs of ice and the glass.

The photograph received wide national play and was later printed in *Life* magazine as a classic publicity picture. Like so much of the photography of the time, this image was made with a large format camera. The 4 × 5 negative size was favored in the newspaper industry because the sheets of film could be developed individually and quickly, and negatives were large enough to reproduce detail and make any necessary retouching easier. It

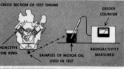

One of Winston Link's first serious photographic subjects was his documentation of the construction of the Triborough Bridge that connect New York City's boroughs of the Bronx, Queens, and Manhattan. This dramatic photograph of the cable-spinning process was made in about 1933. The Hell Gate Bridge over an arm of the East River is seen in the background.

was this large-camera technique that Link was to perfect and which was to be so important in structuring the photographs he was to make of the Norfolk and Western.

In addition to his inventive photographs, Link became famous for his practical jokes at Byoir, mischief which most effectively pinpointed the foibles of its victims. One of his favorites involved a number of Byoir's account executives who were known for such expansive entertainment of their clients that it led on to sometimes forgetful behavior. Over the space of several weeks Link collected blank personalized memo paper from each person's desk. He then typed a rather cavalier invitation to Thanksgiving dinner on each one: "Dear Winston, my wife and I invited fourteen people for Thanksgiving dinner but one of them has disappointed us. Rather than have thirteen at the table we thought we would invite you." Link jotted a response on the bottom of each note politely declining the invitation and returned them to the executives. Pandemonium ensued. Secretaries of several of the men called their wives to let them know that Winston Link could not come to Thanksgiving dinner. This created a panic as the men and their wives wondered that if Winston couldn't come, who else might have been invited? He particularly enjoyed springing such capers on those in the company who enjoyed the give and take of a good practical joke—and that included the firm's general manager. For years after he left Byoir, Link would send this man objects he found flattened in the roadway, ranging from garbage can lids to a long-dead snake.

The young photographer had a number of lady friends, but none was to really catch his fancy until he took a trip south. Carl Byoir had a number of accounts in Texas and Louisiana. Freeport Sulphur Company, then headquartered in Manhattan, operated huge sulphur mining operations in those states. Link traveled to Louisiana on a number of occasions and on one of these trips met Marteal Oglesby, a young model and actress. From that point on he returned as often as he could and Link and Marteal were married in 1942.

That year also marked Link's fifth year at Carl Byoir, where by this time he had built a well-run photography department. But the United States had entered World War II and the photographer wished to serve his country more directly than by working in a public relations agency. A bout with mumps in adolescence had left him almost totally deaf in one ear, making him ineligible for military service, but a friend directed him to what was the perfect wartime job. Columbia University's Office of Scientific Research and Development, a World War II research arm of the university under contract to the military, had created the Airborne Instruments Laboratory in Mineola, Long Island. The lab was seeking a project engineer and photographer. Link's background was exactly right. He was hired in 1942 and Winston and Marteal moved to nearby Hempstead.

The major project of the laboratory was the development of a magnetic airborne detector, a device for the detection of enemy submarines. It was used by trailing a detection pod or "bird" behind an airplane that flew a few feet above the ocean. When the device passed over a large metal object beneath the surface, a sudden change in magnetic flux was registered on a meter in the plane's cockpit. Link polished his skills in creating accurate documentary images of the lab's inventions through the mastery of large-format photography. He used 8 × 10 inch view cameras for his work, and was required on occasion to make photographs at night using flash or flood lights.

One other aspect of working at the lab was to prove of long lasting importance to Winston. The research facilities backed up

to the tracks of the Long Island Rail Road, which was steam-powered at that point on the line. Link began to renew his interest in trains, an interest that had been largely dormant since high school. First he started by creating his own timetable, jotting down the times as the trains passed by. Then he began to photograph the locomotives and trains. He had to do this surreptitiously, for it was against wartime regulations to photograph railroads. Winston worked either from the overpass of the nearby Long Island Motor Parkway, or underneath it, out of sight of the police. These were modest photos, but they fanned his interest in railroads, an interest that was never to go dormant again.

In 1945 Marteal and Winston Link had their only child, a son, Winston Conway Link. But the marriage was in trouble; the couple separated in 1947 and divorced a year later. The year 1945 also saw the end of the war, and the end of Winston's employment at the Airborne Instruments Laboratory. Byoir invited him back but Link decided to go it alone and open his own studio. The past eight years had prepared him well. He had refined a style of studio photography: the use of large cameras, carefully controlled lighting, and the precise placement of people and objects in the creation of images that were directed and controlled by the photographer. Winston's fraternity magazine described it well when they said of his work that "A photographer for a publicity corporation must know how to make posed pictures appear as spot news 'shots.' " The work for Carl Byoir addressed his aptitudes as a dramatist, working with people and having their activities in the photographs not only make sense, but appear to be spontaneous and without artifice. His research at the Airborne Instruments Laboratory addressed the other side of his personality, the precise needs of problem solving and the translation of information into usable photographic documents.

The two sensibilities shaped Link's mature style.

In 1946, Link started his own practice. First he worked out of his house in Hempstead, but after his wife and child left for Louisiana he moved back into his parents' Brooklyn house, soliciting business and making photographs by day and developing and printing at night in a friend's darkroom. It was hard work, but he built up a group of clients that included some of the biggest names in American industry, including B. F. Goodrich, Alcoa Aluminum, Texaco, and Ethyl Corporation. In addition, a number of advertising agencies frequently used his services when they required photos of exceptional technical finesse.

Business grew, and in 1949 he took a floor-through studio in an old building on East Thirty-Fourth Street in Manhattan. Yet Link never expanded his operation beyond himself and one or two part-time assistants. "I had no desire to be big," he has said. "I just wanted to be able to do what I wanted to do. I was happy with what I was doing and happy with the accounts I had, and I liked most of the people I was working for. I wanted to take pictures—not manage a lot of people." It was the ideal job for him. "I wasn't running a business, I was doing something that I liked and I managed to get paid for it. I was lucky." He tried to pick and choose his clients, and enjoyed working with those who were candid about needing his eye, those who would tell him, "I don't know what I want, but I want you to get it! When I see it—I'll know if it's what I thought I wanted."

If it was such a good life, why did Link take on the overwhelming job of documenting the Norfolk and Western, a job that offered no commercial remuneration and only modest professional recognition? Just as he cannot answer the question of how he learned to compose his photos so well, Winston Link cannot precisely answer this question.

One may speculate, however, on several of the reasons. Surely an important factor was that the railroad offered him a field in which he could create a complete work of art in exactly the way he wished to do it, without any commercial intervention. The project thus offered the opportunity to respond to his sensibilities as an artist who had the ambition and the ability to create independently, to reach for something more than being a "hired camera." It allowed him to direct and create his photographs to meet his own standards. The project also permitted him to be a vicarious actor as well as a director, as he planned the photos and worked with the people who would populate them.

There were also no family demands that might have distracted him from the project. He lived simply, and the documentation of the railroad controlled both his professional and personal life at the time. During the years of the project, the Christmas season would find him along the railroad, when heavy passenger traffic required extra sections on the line. For Winston more trains meant more opportunities to photograph. The railroad was his home. It began to seem as if he only camped out in New York while he raised money and planned the next trip.

The people he met while working along the rails became his surrogate family. They were deeply important to him and he would look forward eagerly to making each trip to the south so that he could visit with them. Each person had a story, and the stories piled up. One may also speculate that Winston Link took on the job as a way of answering his father's precepts that one should live one's life in a principled manner and serve humankind valuably. This was another thing that took hold in Winston Link's life. To my way of thinking, it was this gentle but persistent guidance by the senior Link that, years after the fact, helped to provide the psychic drive that gave the photographer the energy to carry forth this huge task.

Certainly, had he not created this personal record, Winston Link would have enjoyed a solid but unremarkable career, creating competent but basically anonymous photographs. He would have been working as that camera for hire, making images, no matter how good, on the instruction of others and for others' use. By creating this document of the Norfolk and Western Railway he transcended the commercial purposes of the rest of his work. Yet he drew upon the disciplines it imposed for accuracy, clarity, and drama in the creation of his personal and poetic statement about the nature of machines and life in America.

These photographs are, in every way, works of art. Winston Link innately possessed what has been called photographic vision, the ability to visualize photographs before they are created and to recognize in the process that what one sees, no matter how interesting, does not necessarily translate into an interesting photograph. The thing photographed and a photograph of it are coequal neither in interest, nor in appearance.

Much of what Winston Link "knew" was there as much by intuition as by instruction or experience. As he says: "I never worked for a photographer, or studied with a photographer. I worked with photographers and I learned from them and they learned from me." His father, however, did leave him with several important lessons which were well learned: "My father taught me the importance of accuracy, patience, consideration of others, honesty, and economy in use of materials." His father also taught Winston to despise greed, avarice, and slipshod work and to love trees and clean water. But Winston Link recalls one other lesson, an important one, and barks out the famous Link laugh as he says "I learned humor from my father too, because so much of everything else in life is just plain bull!"

# AUTHOR'S ACKNOWLEDGMENTS

I have been very fortunate to have known Winston Link for nearly forty years. I met him when I moved to New York following graduation from college. I was studying, needed some part-time work, and was lucky enough to be his assistant for about a year, from September, 1957 to August, 1958. During that time I made three trips with him to the Norfolk and Western to make photographs and tape recordings.

It has been an ambition of mine for years to write the text of another book of Winston's railroad photographs, one that would emphasize his vision and unique contributions to photography, and I am gratified that he trusted me with the task. Just as he learned so much from his father, I have learned so much from him. I am grateful that I have the opportunity now to tell a wider audience about Winston, but believe me, the tale told here just scratches the surface, for the Winston Link stories are endless.

I am also grateful to two railroad men for helping me with specific parts of the text. Donlan Piedmont, retired director of the public affairs department at the Norfolk and Southern Corporation (successor to the Norfolk and Western Railway), who worked for the N&W well before the merger, answered a number of technical questions about personnel and operations and lent me a rare copy of the railroad's history.

Lloyd Lewis, an employee of the CSX Corporation, is the son of a lifelong railroad man who was born near White Top, Virginia and who worked briefly on the Abingdon Branch. Lewis's grandfather helped to build the Abingdon Branch in the early part of the century before it was owned by the N&W. Lloyd Lewis wrote a thoughtful and technically complete article on the Abingdon Branch in the June, 1984, edition of *Trains* magazine, and provided me with additional information about its operations and complicated topography.

Bob Morton, Director of Special Projects for Harry N. Abrams, guided this project and edited the text and photographs with imperturbable skill and great economy of means, for which he has the warmest thanks of both Winston and myself.

Gregory Conniff of Madison, Wisconsin, photographer, thinker, and writer, read an earlier version of this text and offered several key suggestions that substantially improved its content.

Joan Thomas took me in on my two visits to Roanoke, Virginia, to work with Winston on this book. Her kindness gives a whole new meaning to the phrase "southern hospitality."

Mary Bachmann aided both Winston and myself through her very capable assistance both in and out of the darkroom.

Finally, I must thank Natasha Nicholson, my wife, for putting up with me (and this book) as I shuffled photos and hunched over the computer during the year it took to assemble it.

Thomas H. Garver
Madison, Wisconsin